NIGERIA
in Pictures

Janice Hamilton

Lerner Publications Company

Contents

Lerner Publishing Group realizes that current information and statistics quickly become out of date. To extend the usefulness of the Visual Geography Series, we developed www.vgsbooks.com, a website offering links to up-to-date information, as well as in-depth material, on a wide variety of subjects. All of the websites listed on www.vgsbooks.com have been carefully selected by researchers at Lerner Publishing Group. However, Lerner Publishing Group is not responsible for the accuracy or suitability of the material on any website other than <www.lernerbooks.com>. It is recommended that students using the Internet be supervised by a parent or teacher. Links on www.vgsbooks.com will be regularly reviewed and updated as needed.

Website address: www.lernerbooks.com

Lerner Publications Company
A division of Lerner Publishing Group
241 First Avenue North
Minneapolis, MN 55401 U.S.A.

web enhanced @ www.vgsbooks.com

Library of Congress Cataloging-in-Publication Data

Hamilton, Janice.
    Nigeria in pictures / by Janice Hamilton—Rev. and expanded.
      p.   cm. — (Visual geography series)
    Includes bibliographical references and index.
    Summary: Introduces the land, history, government, culture, people, and economy of Nigeria.
    ISBN: 0-8225-0373-5 (lib. bdg. : alk. paper)
    1. Nigeria—Juvenile literature. 2. Nigeria—Pictorial works—Juvenile literature. [1. Nigeria] I. Nigeria in pictures. II. Title. III. Visual geography series (Minneapolis, Minn.)
DT515.22.H36 2003
966.9—dc21   2002005787

Manufactured in the United States of America
1 2 3 4 5 6 - JR - 08 07 06 05 04 03

INTRODUCTION

Nigeria is called the giant of Africa for good reason. With an estimated 129.9 million people, it has the largest population of any African country.

Located just north of the equator in West Africa, the Federal Republic of Nigeria has tropical or subtropical temperatures year-round. There is a wet season and a dry season, but they vary from south to north. Southern Nigeria is humid, and the climate becomes progressively drier in the north. The country's major geographic features include dry grasslands and plateaus in the north and moist, low-lying farmland and forests in the south. Also in the south is a large, Y-shaped valley carved by the Niger and Benue Rivers. The resulting Niger Delta is a vast region of swamps, streams, and lagoons.

The country has a wealth of natural resources, particularly oil and natural gas reserves in the delta and offshore, as well as good agricultural land. Most Nigerians live in rural areas and do at least some farming. Agricultural goods that are produced and used domestically

include yams, cassavas, and cattle, while cocoa, palm oil, and rubber are exported.

Despite the land's natural riches, more than half of Nigerians live in poverty. Services such as electricity, telephone, and clean water are generally unreliable or nonexistent, even in big cities. The quality of life is decreased by environmental concerns, such as pollution from the oil industry, deforestation, and desertification (the transformation of arable land into desert). Education and health services are poor, and HIV/AIDS is a very serious problem.

Nigeria's people are ethnically diverse, with more than 250 different ethnic groups, including the primarily Islamic Hausa and Fulani in the north, the mainly Christian Igbo in the southeast, and the Yoruba, who blend Christianity and Islam, in the southwest. Nigeria's middle belt, a band stretching from east to west across the country's central plateau, is the most diverse area of the country. This region is home to more than half of Nigeria's ethnic groups.

Africa's giant has a long history. Archaeological evidence suggests that several sophisticated ancient civilizations existed in this region as early as five thousand years ago. Later, Islamic traders from North Africa introduced Islam into the area. Between 1481 and 1870, Nigeria played a major role in the Atlantic slave trade, with millions of slaves shipped to Europe, and later to the Americas, from its ports. After the slave trade ended, the British became interested in Nigeria for its natural resources and its rich supply of palm oil. In 1914 Nigeria officially became a British colony.

The country gained independence in 1960 with great hopes for a bright future. Nigeria, however, spent most of the next thirty-nine years under military rule. Following the election of a new civilian government in 1999, the nation still faces problems including corruption and an economy that is overly dependent on oil. Chronic ethnic and religious tensions have intensified since state governments in the north chose to impose Sharia, or Islamic law. In the oil-rich delta, people complain they have not received their fair share of the country's wealth.

Nigerians hope that their government will not only succeed in resolving ethnic and religious differences but also in improving living standards for all of the country's people. The success of democracy in Nigeria may depend upon it.

Nigerians vote to have a say in their government and future. Many Nigerians hope that democratically elected officials will improve conditions in Nigeria.

THE LAND

Nigeria is located just north of the equator, at the point where Africa's Atlantic coastline makes a sharp turn to the west toward the bulge known as West Africa. With a total area of 356,669 square miles (923,772 square kilometers)—slightly more than twice the size of California—the nation shares borders with Benin, Niger, Chad, and Cameroon. Its 530-mile-long (853-km) coast faces the Gulf of Guinea (part of the Atlantic Ocean), including two large bays, the Bight of Benin and the Bight of Bonny (formerly known as the Bight of Biafra).

Topography

Nigeria has a wide variety of landscapes, climates, and ecological zones. Low, swampy plains dominate the coast from the city of Lagos, across the Niger Delta (the mouth of the Niger River), to the Cameroon border. Throughout this area lie deposits of mud, clay, and sand, along with a myriad of streams, rivers, and lagoons.

Mangrove trees thrive in the brackish water (a mix of saltwater and freshwater), and the mangrove forest extends between 9 and 30 miles (14 and 48 km) inland from the coast. Then the forest of the freshwater swamp takes over, with a tangle of trees with stilted roots, climbing palms with hooked spines, and nearly impenetrable shrubs.

Inland from the delta is a densely populated east-west band with many farms and tree plantations. This region was once part of the lowland rain forest zone, though much of this forest has disappeared. A few large pockets of forested land remain in game reserves and parks.

Moving northward, the land rises and rainfall declines. The Western Uplands is a high grassland dotted with granite ridges and inselbergs (isolated rock domes). The valley of the Niger and Benue Rivers crosses central Nigeria in a large "Y" as the two rivers join forces and run south to the delta. They flow through a variety of landscapes, from rocky hills to grasslands, forests, and swamps.

Most of the Eastern Highlands, lying along the Cameroon border, are 4,000 feet (1,219 meters) or more above sea level. Dimlang Peak, the country's highest point at 6,699 feet (2,042 m) above sea level, is part of this region. On the mist-shrouded lower slopes, mosses and epiphytes (plants that get moisture from the air) thrive among the damp trees. Higher up, the trees disappear and only grasses grow.

The Northern High Plains, with their outcroppings of volcanic rock, cover about one-fifth of Nigeria. The Guinea Savanna ecological zone dominates this middle belt of the country, and woodlands and shrubs are typical. Tall grasses thrive in open zones. Since grass fires are common in the dry season, most trees have thick, fire-resistant bark and send up new shoots after being burned.

The central Jos Plateau, which rises out of the Northern High Plains, has scenic rocky hills reaching about 5,000 feet (1,524 m) above sea level. This distinct ecological zone is home to some species of orchids and other plants found nowhere else in West Africa. But human activities have had a huge impact on the vegetation, and the area is almost treeless.

Much of northern Nigeria is part of an ecological zone known as the Sudan Savanna. Grasses are short and feathery, and trees are few, though there are lots of thorny acacia shrubs. The Chad Basin around Lake Chad is marshy in the rainy season but becomes parched during seasons of drought. The northeastern corner of Nigeria is part of the Sahel, a vast, dry grassland that forms a transition zone between the Sahara Desert and the more humid savanna.

The word *sahel* means fringe or edge. Nigeria's Sahel is a hot, dry region located between the edges of the Sahara Desert and the Sudan Savanna.

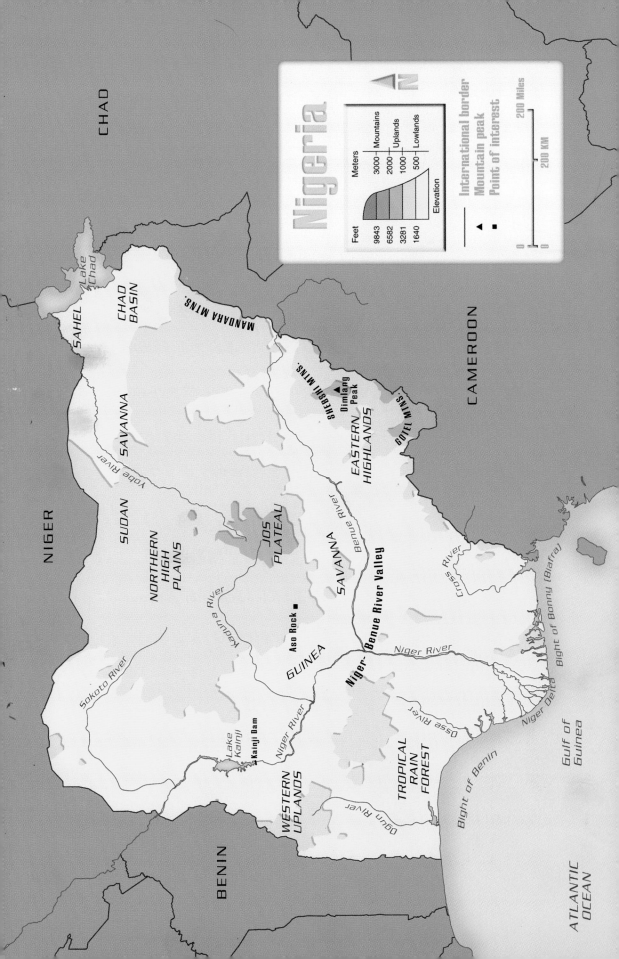

CHAD

NIGER

BENIN

CAMEROON

ATLANTIC
OCEAN

Nigeria

Meters   Feet
3000 — Mountains   9843
2000 — Uplands   6582
1000 —   3281
500 — Lowlands   1640

Elevation

International border
▲ Mountain peak
■ Point of interest

0 ─────────── 200 Miles
0 ─────────── 200 KM

SAHEL

Lake
Chad

CHAD
BASIN

MANDARA MTNS.

SAVANNA

Yobe River

SUDAN

NORTHERN
HIGH
PLAINS

JOS
PLATEAU

SHEBSHI MTNS.

▲ Dimlang
Peak

EASTERN
HIGHLANDS

GOTEL MTNS.

Benue River

SAVANNA

Niger- Benue River Valley

Cross River

Kaduna River

Sokoto River

GUINEA

■ Aso Rock

Niger River

Niger River

Ossè River

TROPICAL
RAIN
FOREST

Niger Delta

Bight of Bonny (Biafra)

Lake
Kainji

Kainji Dam

WESTERN
UPLANDS

Ogun River

Bight of Benin

Gulf of
Guinea

Nigeria's lush, wet **tropical rain forest** located in the southern part of the country contrasts sharply with the arid regions of northern Nigeria.

Climate

Nigeria has two seasons: the wet season and the dry season. They are influenced by monsoon winds, which carry moisture from the Atlantic Ocean in the southwest, and by a dry wind, called the *harmattan*, which blows from the Sahara in the northeast.

The seasons vary from south to north in timing, precipitation, and duration. In the south, the rainy season lasts most of the year, and humidity levels can be very uncomfortable. The southeastern coast and the Niger Delta receive the most rain, getting between 78 and 118 inches (198 and 300 centimeters) a year. Inland, the rainy season begins in April, May, or June, starting progressively later toward the north. By August, rainfall is at its peak everywhere.

Northeast winds bring clear skies from September through November. Then, from December to February, the strong winds of the harmattan carry fine Saharan dust that covers everything. The harmattan primarily affects northern Nigeria, but in some years it blows far into the south. In coastal Lagos, average temperatures are 81° F (27° C) in January and 78° F (25° C) in July, while in the northern city of Kano they are 70° F (21° C) and 79° F (26° C), respectively.

Rivers and Lakes

The 2,600-mile-long (4,184-km) Niger River is Africa's third largest river after the Nile and the Congo. The final one-third of its course is in Nigeria. Shortly after crossing from Benin into Nigeria, it is joined by several tributaries, including the Sokoto and Kaduna, and flows into a human-made reservoir behind the Kainji Dam. Its largest tributary, the Benue River, originates in the mountains of Cameroon and joins the Niger near the town of Lokoja. The Niger then flows through narrow valleys and across flat plains. It divides into the many channels and streams of the delta and finally empties into the Gulf of Guinea along a 200-mile (322-km) stretch of coastline.

The name Nigeria stems from the name of the country's great river. The name was coined in 1898 by Flora Shaw, a British journalist. Even after British colonization of Nigeria ended, Nigerians kept the name, honoring the river that is the lifeblood of the nation.

The Niger River is critical to Nigerian life. It yields large catches of fish and provides water for millions of people. But droughts and an increased demand for water from a growing population have decreased the river's water level. The problem is aggravated by the eroded soil that washes into the river and chokes the river's flow.

Northwest of the delta, several short rivers including the Ogun and Osse flow into the Bight of Benin, while in the southeast, the Cross River is the main waterway. In the northeast, the Yobe, with tributaries draining the Northern High Plains, flows into Lake Chad.

The Niger River is a lifeline for people, animals, and plants. The Niger is threatened by increasing demands on its valuable water resources.

Large mammals, such as hippos and **giraffes,** once roamed freely in great numbers in Nigeria. Poaching and land development for cities and farms have reduced their numbers. Only a fraction of the former herds still exist, mainly living within wildlife reserves. For links to photos and more information on African wildlife, go to vgsbooks.com.

This lake, lying on the border between Nigeria, Niger, Chad, and Cameroon, is the remnant of an ancient sea. It is one of Africa's largest lakes, but its size varies considerably from season to season.

Wildlife

Estimates of the number of bird species identified in Nigeria vary, but at least several hundred seasonal migrants from Europe have been spotted, in addition to other species that are found only in this region. Guinea fowl, quail, and vultures live on the savanna, while hornbills prefer forests and woodlands. At least nine species of birds and twenty-six mammal species, including the cheetah and the pygmy hippopotamus, are listed as critically endangered, endangered, or vulnerable. Most large mammals are no longer found in abundance because of over-hunting and habitat destruction. About two dozen antelope species, including duikers, roan antelopes, and water bucks, are found on the savanna, although rarely in huge herds. Primates, such as baboons and chimpanzees, and large cats, such as lions and leopards, are restricted to game reserves.

Nigeria's swamps and creeks are home to water snakes, turtles, frogs, ghost crabs, hairy mangrove crabs, and many species of fish.

Three species of crocodile, including the dangerous Nile crocodile, are found in the Niger and its tributaries.

Natural Resources

The country's most abundant and economically important resource by far is petroleum. Nigeria is one of the world's major oil-producing countries, with proven reserves of 22.5 billion barrels. Much of this oil lies under the swamps of the delta. Nigeria also has vast quantities of natural gas and coal.

Nigeria is an important producer of tin and of columbite, a mineral used in the production of some types of steel. There are more than 3.3 billion tons (3 billion metric tons) of iron-ore deposits in the middle belt, along with lead, zinc, limestone, marble, and feldspar. Gold has been discovered in several areas, and there are plans to use uranium deposits.

Around 75 percent of the country's total landmass is suitable for agriculture, including farming, forestry, livestock raising, and fish farming. The north is the main crop-growing area. Almost half of the country's fishery resources come from coastal waters, with the remainder supplied by Nigeria's rivers and lakes.

Nigeria has many native species of trees, some of which are important resources. Edible coconut palms are found along beaches and lagoons, and the oil palm provides palm oil and palm wine. In coastal regions, the red mangrove, so named because of its smooth, pinkish gray bark, is used for fuel. Economically important rain forest trees include ebony and mahogany, while the tall, deciduous iroko, valuable for its strong brown timber, provides much of the country's export wood.

Environmental Challenges

Rapid population growth and exploitation of natural resources have created environmental problems in Nigeria. One of the most serious of these challenges is oil pollution in the delta. In the north, deforestation and desertification present additional problems.

The 42,000-square-mile (108,780-sq.-km) Niger Delta, one of the world's largest wetlands, is home to seven million people belonging to thirteen different ethnic groups. It is also the source of most of the 2 million barrels of oil that Nigeria produces every day. No one really knows how much oil has polluted this area. One study estimates that between 1986 and 1996, spills leaked at least 2.5 million barrels of oil into the environment, destroying much of the area's farmland and killing fish and wildlife. In addition, for many years the natural gas that is found with oil has been deliberately burned off because there were no facilities to sell it. This flaring, or burning off, lit up the night sky, creating acid rain and contributing to global warming.

The environmental struggles have increased political unrest and violence. Residents—angered by the terrible pollution and by the lack of jobs, roads, bridges, schools, electricity, and other services in this poverty-stricken region—sometimes kidnap oil company employees or sabotage oil wells, creating more pollution.

Some steps are being taken to solve these problems. The federal government has promised to pump more funds into delta communities. Some oil companies have tried to help the villagers by building roads and schools. There are plans to eliminate flaring and to turn the natural gas into fertilizer or fuel. But the government also intends to increase oil production to 3 million barrels a day by 2003, and critics say environmental regulations are inadequate to handle the output.

Deforestation is another ongoing problem, and trees have been almost wiped out in some areas. This, in turn, has led to increasing desertification, especially in areas with poor soil to begin with. Bad irrigation practices, overgrazing, and the overuse of poor agricultural land also contribute to desertification. In 2001 the federal government announced a plan to fight both problems by planting millions of tree seedlings along a 930-mile-long (1,496-km) belt through northern Nigeria. New trees will provide a wind barrier, will help stabilize the fragile soil, and will halt the movement of sand dunes.

◉ Cities

LAGOS is Nigeria's largest city, port, and commercial center. This crowded metropolis has an estimated urban area population of 12.8 million residents. A melting pot of Nigeria's ethnic groups, it is one of the fastest growing cities in the world, drawing about 300,000 newcomers every year. Lagos offers a range of attractions including museums, theaters, a stadium, and nearby beaches. Its inhabitants are known for their sheer energy and ingenuity. Among the city's problems are poverty, pollution, crime, and traffic jams. Sprawling across four main islands and the shores of a lagoon, Lagos has a busy port. Major industries include automobile assembly, food and beverage processing, and pharmaceutical manufacturing.

Lagos's history began with an early Yoruba settlement on Lagos Island. From the late 1500s to the mid-1800s, the Kingdom of Benin dominated the region. The British took control of Lagos in 1861, and nearly a century later it became Nigeria's capital.

ABUJA became the federal capital of Nigeria in 1991. The new capital boasts sparkling government office buildings, law courts, conference centers, mosques (Islamic places of prayer), hotels, and an international airport. Forming a crescent shape at the foot of Aso Rock, Abuja has an estimated population of 500,000 .

IBADAN'S population is an estimated 1.4 million. However, censuses in Nigeria are infrequent and often inaccurate, and some estimates put Ibadan's population at more than 5 million. This Yoruba city is famous for its university, as well as for textile dyeing and pottery making. Many residents are part-time farmers, and there are dozens of small commercial stalls and markets in the heart of the city.

KANO is Nigeria's oldest city. It was the capital of a Hausa state in the 1100s, and in the nineteenth century it was an important market town and the capital of an emirate (an Islamic state). Present-day Kano, with an estimated 657,000 residents, most of them Hausa and Fulani, remains an important commercial and industrial city.

ENUGU, a sprawling Igbo city, is another major urban center. The city is in the heart of Nigeria's coal-mining region as well as a productive agricultural center.

PORT HARCOURT, with oil fields and refineries, has the second-largest seaport in the country. Jos, a small city founded on tin mining and tourism, and Calabar, a busy fishing port and once a slave trade center, are other important Nigerian cities.

> Lagos is infamous for its "go-slows," or traffic tie-ups. Everyone who can afford it uses a car, even for short distances, and street merchants, selling everything from smoked fish to toilet brushes, take advantage of the go-slows to sell their wares to immobilized customers.

Pedestrians, drivers, and street vendors fill a busy street in the **city of Lagos.**

HISTORY AND GOVERNMENT

Humans have lived in the area known as Nigeria for a long time. Archaeologists have found ancient stone tools in the region, along with a human skeleton from about 9000 B.C. The first societies in Nigeria formed about 3000 B.C. Nigeria's earliest inhabitants were hunters and gatherers. People living on the edge of the country's forests learned to grow their own food in about 1000 B.C., using stone axes imported from the north to clear the forest so that they could grow yams.

These early Nigerians made several important contributions to African culture. The Benue Valley was the birthplace of Bantu, the largest branch of the Niger-Congo language family, one of four groups of African languages.

The people of this region were also among the first in sub-Saharan Africa to adopt iron technology, making iron hoes for agriculture, axes for cutting trees, and tools for digging wells and irrigation works. Archaeologists have found the remains of iron-smelting furnaces from

around 450 B.C. at Taruga on the Jos Plateau. This site belonged to the Nok culture, the first advanced civilization known to exist in the area. It flourished in a large area of central Nigeria from about 500 B.C. to A.D. 200 and is best known for its stylized terra-cotta figurines.

City-States and Kingdoms

Trade in the region grew in importance after about A.D. 700. Caravans of traders from North Africa crossed the Sahara by camel, bringing pottery, glass, and salt, which they exchanged for ivory, ebony, gold, and slaves. Closer to home, people from the forested regions of southern Nigeria began to trade with brokers from the Sahel and the savanna regions. As the people of the region became wealthy, they wanted more luxury goods and began to specialize in a variety of crafts. Towns, city-states, and kingdoms developed throughout the region after A.D. 1000. Meanwhile, merchants from the north had brought Islam to West Africa.

By the 1200s, an Islamic ethnic group called the Hausa had built several walled cities on the Sahel, including Kano, Katsina, Zaria, and Gobir. Because they were centrally located, these settlements became important commercial hubs. Local artisans made leatherwork, textiles, and other products. Ivory, gold, and slaves from the south passed through their markets, while salt and other goods from the Mediterranean came from the north. Kano also became a renowned center for Islamic scholarship and piety.

To the southwest, the Yoruba people established the city of Ife. Ife was known for its bronze sculptures. It was also the center of several hundred cults, or religions. In the fifteenth century, Ife remained a religious center, but two other kingdoms, Oyo and Benin, became more important as political and commercial city-states. Oyo, north of Ife in the savanna, developed busy trade connections. Copper, textiles, leather goods, and horses came from the north, and kola nuts, indigo (a blue dye), parrots, and cowrie shells came from the south.

The oldest section of Kano's Old City is almost one thousand years old. Several **ancient gates** still stand, remnants of a thick mud wall that used to surround the city.

The people of Ife once used the lost wax process to create beautiful **bronze sculptures** like this head of an unknown leader. A model was made of wax and placed between two layers of clay. After the clay dried and hardened, the wax was melted and removed. Molten bronze was then poured into the clay mold.

The Edo-speaking people of the Kingdom of Benin, east of Ife, also gained prominence in the 1400s. The Benin *oba*, or political and religious leader, was a powerful figure. The Kingdom of Benin controlled parts of Yoruba and Igbo territories stretching from the recently established city of Lagos to the Nile. Benin's traders were hard bargainers, and its merchants became wealthy trading iron tools, weapons, and food products. Its craftspeople created bronze plaques and sculptures illustrating daily life in Benin's royal courts. The bronzes depicted hunting expeditions, festivals, and highly disciplined warriors.

Other ethnic groups, including the Igbo, did not form centralized states. Instead, the citizens of each Igbo community met together to make important decisions.

In the sixteenth century, the vast Songhai Empire, stretching from the Gambia and Senegal Rivers in the west to Hausaland in the east, dominated northwestern Nigeria culturally and economically. The Songhai Empire's influence disappeared in 1591, when it was conquered by invaders from Morocco. In the northeast, near Lake Chad, the Bornu Empire reached its peak in the late 1500s after growing prosperous through the desert trade. Although its rulers were Islamic, they also maintained many traditional African practices.

With the fall of Songhai, Bornu dominated several Hausa cities, including Katsina and Kano, for almost two hundred years. Severe drought brought famine in the 1740s and 1750s, and camel-riding Tuareg warriors from central Nigeria took over some of Bornu's weakened territories.

The Atlantic Slave Trade

At the same time that city-states were developing within the region, a new and powerful external influence began to affect Nigeria. By 1436 Portuguese ships had begun exploring the coast of West Africa, looking for riches. In 1471 they ventured as far south as the Niger Delta, and ten years later they sent a delegation to the court of Benin's oba.

Soon European traders were conducting a steady business in Africa, exchanging cloth, beads, copper and brass *manillas* (bracelets), and other goods for gold, ivory, pepper, and slaves. They sent the slaves to Portugal, to sugar plantations on Madeira and the Cape Verde Islands, and to the Gold Coast (present-day Ghana). Later, male slaves were shipped abroad to work in the sugarcane fields of the Americas, while most female slaves were sold in Africa as agricultural and domestic workers and to bear children. In the course of the Atlantic slave trade, at least nine or ten million African slaves arrived in the Americas, and an estimated one million more died en route. The true totals may be even higher.

A Portuguese slave trader *(left)* watches over a group of enslaved Africans destined for Nigeria's Slave Coast and a life of forced labor. Visit vgsbooks.com to find out more about slavery.

Most African slaves came from western and central Africa, and the coast of present-day Nigeria became known as the Slave Coast. Ports from Lagos to Calabar acted as transfer points for slaves bound for the Caribbean and North and South America. Some 3.5 million slaves, including Yoruba, Igbo, Ibibio, Hausa, and individuals from other ethnic groups, were shipped abroad from Nigeria, primarily to the United States, Cuba, and Brazil.

Slavery was not new in Africa. Many societies had slaves from other ethnic groups, and some groups punished criminals by selling them into slavery. When the Atlantic trade began, many African slave merchants became very wealthy. As the slave trade grew in scope and importance, the Yoruba of Oyo, the Aro, the coastal Ijaw, and the Efik were especially busy. They captured or bought slaves and then sold them to the Europeans.

SLAVERY IN AFRICA

Slavery had been common in Africa for thousands of years before the Atlantic trade began. However, groups regarded slaves differently and used them for different purposes. Some cultures, including the Kingdom of Benin, put slaves to death as sacrifices. Others bought slaves to be servants. Some slaves with special skills acquired trusted positions and economic power. Second generations of slaves were sometimes regarded as free members of the community. Islamic societies such as the Songhai Empire had large numbers of slaves, primarily as domestic servants.

As the sixteenth century drew to a close, the Dutch challenged Portuguese dominance in the slave trade and took over their trading stations. By the 1700s, the British were dominant. One of the many consequences of the Atlantic slave trade was the deprivation of West African communities of needed workers. The trade also contributed to bitterness among ethnic groups and created a demand for new goods such as rum, guns, and gunpowder that the trade introduced to the region.

Sokoto Caliphate and Yoruba Wars

Early in the 1800s, important events swept through northern Nigeria. An influential cleric named Usman dan Fodio became the leader of a group of devout Islamic Fulani. These Fulani were upset that, although local rulers were Muslims (followers of Islam), they allowed the common people to practice some traditional African religions. The group also wanted these rulers to observe Islamic laws fully. In 1804 Usman and his followers prepared to lead a revolutionary jihad, or holy war, to overthrow the old rulers and to bring about these and other changes.

By 1809 Usman had overthrown the Hausa states and had established the Sokoto Caliphate (a religious state), with a capital at the newly founded city of Sokoto. The rulers of member emirates (states led by rulers called emirs) pledged loyalty to the caliph (leader) and made financial contributions to Sokoto, while the caliphate oversaw disputes between emirates. By the mid-1800s, the Sokoto Caliphate stretched for more than 930 miles (1,500 km), from present-day Burkina Faso to Cameroon.

Changes were also occurring in southern Nigeria at this time. In the early 1800s, Britain had made it illegal for British subjects to take part in the slave trade. The British military established naval blockades off the West African coast to intercept slave ships and to free slaves who had been rescued at sea. Britain's commercial interests in Nigeria turned from slaves to agricultural products, especially palm oil from the wild palm trees that grew abundantly in the delta. Despite the official end of the Atlantic slave trade, slaves still collected palm fruits, extracted the oil, and transported it to the coast.

The Oyo Empire had controlled much of southwestern Nigeria since the 1400s. In the 1820s, the commercial uncertainty resulting from the British withdrawal from the Atlantic slave trade, along with internal power struggles, caused the empire to collapse. Many people left the old site of the Oyo Empire and founded cities such as Ibadan and the new city of Oyo, south of the old capital.

Following this upheaval was an extended period of civil war among the Yoruba, and many captives taken in this war were forced into slavery. In fact, the Atlantic slave trade continued to flourish until the 1860s, despite having been banned by several countries. There was still a strong demand for slaves in Cuba and Brazil, and about one million slaves were exported from Nigeria during the 1800s.

Meanwhile, British efforts to curb slavery, stop the fighting between the Yoruba, and protect their own commercial interests drew Britain into greater involvement in Nigeria. In 1851 British troops attacked Lagos with the goal of expelling the Benin king who ruled the area. When Lagos surrendered, the British placed a ruler on the throne who was sympathetic to the idea of abolishing slavery. In 1861 Britain annexed (took over) Lagos in a first step toward colonization.

In 1879 British businessman George Goldie persuaded several British trading companies to merge, and the resulting United Africa Company established a monopoly over African trade. To reduce the costs of administration of the region, the British government gave administrative responsibility to Goldie's company. Renamed the Royal Niger Company, it built its headquarters at Lokoja.

The Carving Up of Africa

Between 1884 and 1885, representatives of several European nations, including Britain, France, and Germany, attended the Berlin West Africa conference. These nations used the goal of eliminating slavery to justify carving up Africa and dividing the continent among themselves. No Africans were invited to attend the conference. The European powers agreed on where to place the borders between their colonies with little consideration for local concerns or ethnic groups. Their motives had more to do with strategic and commercial ambitions and with a desire to educate and convert Africans to Christianity than with the well-being of the inhabitants. Portuguese Roman Catholic missionaries had first brought Christianity to the Kingdom of Benin. After 1840 more missionaries became active in Nigeria, including Presbyterians, Methodists, Baptists, and the Church of England's Church Missionary Society (CMS).

With a small colony already established in Lagos, the British made the Niger Delta a protectorate (a dependent territory under British control). They placed the area under the management of the British Foreign Office in order to regulate local trade. In 1894 they expanded the protectorate's territory to Lokoja. The British were able to bring some regions under their power through diplomacy, while others, including the Kingdom of Benin, had to be taken by military force.

In 1899 the British government in London decided that a commercial company did not have the expertise to deal with international issues. The Royal Niger Company lost its contract to operate in 1900, and the British set up the Protectorate of Southern Nigeria and the Protectorate of Northern Nigeria. Army officer Frederick Lugard served as high commissioner of the Northern Protectorate from 1900 to 1906 and brought the Sokoto Caliphate under British control. He also implemented a policy called indirect rule, in which the British acted as absentee overlords and the defeated emirs carried out local administration.

The Colony

In 1914 the northern and southern regions were joined, and Lugard became the first governor-general of colonial Nigeria. Although unified, the colony had separate regional administrations. The policy of indirect rule was still used to handle local affairs throughout the colony. In some regions, especially in Igbo territory, the British had trouble finding individuals who were acceptable to them and also recognized as authorities by the local people.

Economic development in Nigeria began with the construction of roads, railroads, and harbors. Progress was more uneven in the area of education, since missionaries who tried to expand both Christianity and British-style education did not have the same access to the strongly Islamic north as they did to the south. The British also brought their legal traditions to Nigeria, and a dual system of British and Islamic law developed in the north. English became the official language of the south, while in the north the Hausa language shared official status with English.

During World War I (1914–1918), Nigerian troops fought in German-held Cameroon. The wartime need for better port and transportation facilities stimulated more improvements in Nigeria. Involvement in the war also inspired political action. A group of Africans from across the continent began to look for ways to end European domination and racism. Local Nigerian leaders demanded greater responsibilities and freedom from colonial rule. In response, the British brought in a series of changes to government structures, including the first elected representatives on the colony's legislative council.

Herbert Macaulay, an African politician who founded Nigeria's first political party in 1923, became known as the father of modern Nigerian nationalism. Student organizations led the nationalist movement, and newspapers helped spread its ideas. In multi-ethnic Nigeria, nationalism had less to do with a belief in a common destiny than in a desire to have more of a voice in regional government. In the north, nationalists wanted to uphold Islamic traditions, while southerners were more interested in throwing off colonial rulers who had historically excluded them from decision making.

Nigerian troops proved their worth again during World War II (1939–1945), fighting alongside the British in East Africa and Burma.

Nigerian soldiers stand for inspection during World War II.

Facing outside pressure to decolonize, Britain began to reassess Nigeria's political future after the war. By this time, the country's main political parties were divided along ethnic lines, and the various groups were jockeying to be in a strong position when independence arrived.

Between 1946 and 1954, the constitution was revised three times, giving the colony greater autonomy. In 1957 the western and eastern regions achieved the right to govern themselves on some matters, and the northern region followed suit two years later.

Independence

Nigeria became independent on October 1, 1960. The new federal government consisted of a parliament with a house of representatives and a senate whose members were chosen by the regional legislatures. The governor-general, who acted as head of state, still officially represented the power of the British monarch.

The first government was a coalition with Alhaji Abubakar Tafawa Balewa, a northerner who had been educated abroad, serving as prime minister. Nnamdi Azikiwe, an Igbo who had been involved in national politics since the 1930s, was governor-general. In 1963 Nigeria became a republic with a president acting as head of state. Elected to a five-year term by the parliament, Azikiwe became the country's first president.

People had high hopes for this newly independent country. Nigeria had the largest population in Africa, experienced politicians and civil servants, and many natural resources. In the period leading up to independence, Nigeria had enjoyed a healthy economy.

GIANT HOPE

When Nigeria became independent in 1960, there were great hopes for its future. One African in six was a Nigerian. The nation had new universities, tarred roads between major towns, refrigerators, Africa's first television station, and plans for a second one. In contrast with some of its neighbors, which had few or no trained specialists, Nigeria had 532 doctors, 644 lawyers, many engineers and accountants, and thousands of experienced civil servants.

Proud students celebrate Nigeria's independence on October 1, 1960.

The country exported oil, cotton, groundnuts (similar to peanuts), cocoa, and palm products. However, rivalries existed among the nation's ethnic groups, and economic and educational differences between the north and the south created additional tension.

In January 1966, a group of army officers attempted a coup (an overthrow of the government). They executed Prime Minister Balewa and two regional officials. An Igbo, Major General Johnson Aguiyi-Ironsi, took power. He planned to set up a military government, but the army itself was split along ethnic lines, and Aguiyi-Ironsi lacked support among the troops. He and other Igbo had adjusted well to colonial rule. They had educated their children and gotten good jobs as doctors, lawyers, army officers, and government officials. In the new republic, some Nigerians resented the Igbo's success and suspected that there had been an Igbo conspiracy to control the country.

In July, northern army officers staged a countercoup. Aguiyi-Ironsi was killed, and Lieutenant Colonel Yakubu Gowon, a Christian northerner, took control. In the north, the resentment felt by Nigerian Muslims erupted into violence against Christians. Thousands of Christian Igbo were killed, and about one million were forced to flee to eastern Nigeria.

◎ The Biafran War

To stem the continuing violence, the federal government tried to ease tensions among the country's four large regions by dividing Nigeria into twelve smaller states. But on May 30, 1967, the military governor Lieutenant Colonel Odumegwu Ojukwu announced that the Eastern Region, which was primarily Igbo, was seceding from Nigeria to become the Republic of Biafra. By July civil war had erupted between Biafra and other regions of Nigeria.

Biafra won some victories in the early days of the war, but soon its forces were beaten back and it was cut off from supplies. The thirty-month war ended when Biafran leaders surrendered in January 1970. It is estimated that about one million people died, most of them from starvation. To make the return to peace smoother, Gowon promised that this war would produce no winners and no losers. Igbo leaders and soldiers were not punished, and many Igbo returned to their former jobs in the army and civil service.

Nigerian leaders promised that the nation would return to civilian rule in 1974. Gowon tried to postpone the changeover, and he was overthrown in 1975. Brigadier Murtala Ramat Mohammed tried to organize a return to democracy, but he was assassinated in 1976 in an unsuccessful coup attempt.

Lieutenant General Olusegun Obasanjo, Mohammed's chief aide, took over. A new constitution was drawn up, replacing the British-style

A mother and child face another day of **hunger** during the Biafran War (1967–1970). Caught between two sides of the bloody civil war and cut off from food supplies, thousands of Nigerians died of starvation.

parliamentary system with an American-style presidential model. The constitution was adopted in 1979, and the Second Republic was born. That same year, a presidential election was held, under military supervision.

The end of the 1970s saw new economic challenges. The decade had been a period of excess in Nigeria. Growing revenues from the sale of petroleum flowed into the country, but the money was often spent on luxury goods for the very rich. The government started to depend on oil revenues and did not bother to invest in other areas of the economy. The high value of the naira, Nigeria's currency, meant that it was cheaper for Nigerians to buy imported food than to buy domestic produce. At the same time, buyers abroad refused to buy Nigerian cocoa, cotton, and groundnuts because they were too expensive. Farmers suffered, plantations were abandoned, and many people moved to the cities. Then oil prices fell, and by the early 1980s the country was heavily in debt.

Military Rule

In 1983 the military staged a coup, saying that the terrible economic conditions and other mistakes made by the civilian leadership justified a military takeover. Pledging to eliminate corruption, the new president arrested political opponents and journalists. But in 1985, another bloodless military coup occurred, this time led by General Ibrahim Babangida.

During the unrest of the 1990s, **author Ken Saro-Wiwa** worked for political, environmental, and social change in Nigeria. He wrote, "I call upon you, my brothers and sisters, to fight relentlessly for your rights. As our cause is just ... we shall emerge victorious."

Babangida tried to control corruption and made ambitious efforts to improve the floundering economy. He declared a national economic emergency, banned luxury imports, cut the budget, and encouraged people to return to farming. Like leaders before him, Babangida vowed that the country would return to democracy. After a series of delays, during which Babangida tried to hold on to power, a presidential election was held in June 1993. Chief Moshood Abiola, a Yoruba Muslim, was the winner.

Babangida claimed that voting mistakes had skewed the results. When he annulled the election, he was forced from office. An interim government took shape, but in November 1993, there was yet another coup. A former minister of defense, General Sani Abacha, assumed power, ushering in one of the darkest periods of Nigerian history.

The Abacha regime jailed political opponents—including president-elect Abiola—restricted freedom of the press, and abused human rights. Abacha abandoned the constitution and ruled as a military dictator, as he and his friends and family stole from the government treasury and collected bribes.

In 1995 one of the Abacha regime's actions received worldwide attention. Writer and activist Ken Saro-Wiwa, head of Mosop (Movement for the Survival of the Ogoni People), campaigned for political autonomy for the Ogoni, an ethnic minority living in the delta region. He also spoke out against the environmental damage caused by the oil companies.

Saro-Wiwa was tried by a military court for ordering the murder of four chiefs who had questioned his confrontational style. After being convicted in an unfair trial, Saro-Wiwa and eight of his supporters were hanged. People around the world sympathized with Saro-Wiwa, and the execution led to Nigeria's suspension from the Commonwealth of former British colonies.

After Abacha died of a heart attack in 1998, General Abdulsalami Abubakar took charge and announced that the military would return the country to civilian rule. A month later, Abiola, who still claimed to be the legitimate president, died shortly before he was to have been released from prison. Riots broke out over Abiola's death—which many Nigerians found suspicious—and over the control of the military government, and things were set in motion for an election. The vote took place in February 1999, and Olusegun Obasanjo—the man who twenty years earlier had turned another military government over to civilian rule—was declared the winner. He was sworn into office on May 29, 1999. A revised constitution took effect, and Nigeria was readmitted to the Commonwealth.

A 1999 **campaign billboard** encourages Nigerians to vote for Olusegun Obasanjo for president. Obasanjo won the election, taking office in May 1999.

A bicyclist rides past the **burned-out remains of a Christian church** in Kano, a reminder of ongoing tensions in Nigeria. The fire was set only days earlier during fighting between Christians and Muslims.

Ongoing Challenges

Obasanjo's government faces many problems, including unrest in Lagos and the oil-rich delta. Violent clashes continue among different ethnic groups, as well as between Muslims and Christians. Estimates of the number of people killed in ethnic and religious violence from 1999 to 2002 range between six thousand and ten thousand. Many Nigerians blame the nation's leaders for failing to prevent these deaths.

The problems in the delta stem from years of isolation, pollution, and neglect. Members of the many small ethnic groups there say they have not received their fair share of the country's wealth or decision-making power. Even though most of Nigeria's income comes from delta oil, only about 3 percent of Nigeria's oil revenue ends up in the delta, and it remains one of the poorest regions in the country. Proposed changes would give the area 13 percent of these revenues.

Another challenge is ongoing ethnic strife. Throughout Nigeria tensions among the many groups are worsening. This trouble also adds to political instability. Since colonial days, most Nigerian political parties have been based more along ethnic lines than along ideological beliefs. Some Yoruba support the Oodua People's Congress (OPC), a militant nationalist organization that is demanding a separate Yoruba state. In the east, some Igbo people feel they are treated like second-class citizens and would like to see the revival of a separate Biafra. The Hausa have organized their own militia group, the Arewa People's Congress (APC). In 2001 dozens of people were killed and at least twenty-five thousand fled their homes after an outbreak of ethnic violence in two central states between Hausa-speaking people and the Tiv ethnic group.

Nigeria has also seen a serious increase in violent clashes between Muslims and Christians. In 2000 religious riots in the state of Kaduna resulted in the burning of mosques and churches and more than two thousand deaths. More riots between religious groups broke out in Jos in 2001. Fanning the fire was the decision by twelve predominantly Islamic states to implement the Islamic legal system, Sharia. Northern Muslims have traditionally applied Sharia to civil cases such as divorce and land disputes. When they began sentencing Muslims to some of Sharia's harsher penalties, such as stoning for adultery and amputation of the hand for theft, non-Islamic Nigerians began to fear that they would also be judged under Sharia. Many Christians and followers of traditional African religions left the north. In 2002 the federal government declared some of Sharia's physical punishments unconstitutional. Northern Islamic states refused to comply with President Obasanjo's demands to change their traditional religious laws. However, to many Muslims, the true issue is less about religious differences than about political power. They support Sharia because they see its clear moral code as a way to clear up Nigeria's corruption and to solve social and economic problems.

◉ Government

The Federal Republic of Nigeria is a federation of thirty-six states and a Federal Capital Territory (at Abuja). The constitution, first put into effect in 1979, has been revised several times. Under the 1999 constitution, the federal government's National Assembly is made up of a popularly elected 109-member senate and a 360-member house of representatives. The assembly is the legislative body, while the president holds executive powers and is head of state. The president is elected for a four-year term.

There are two other levels of government below the federal one. Each of the thirty-six states has a governor, elected for four years, and a state house of assembly. Below the state level, there are 774 local government councils in the country.

Nigeria's judicial branch has a Supreme Court, a Federal Court of Appeal, and several other lower courts. The legal system is based on a combination of British common law, Islamic law, and traditional laws.

Nigeria's motto is "Unity and Faith, Peace and Progress." Visit vgsbooks.com to track current developments in Nigeria, read the constitution and presidential speeches, and find out more about human rights and other challenges facing Nigeria's government.

THE PEOPLE

Nigeria is Africa's most heavily populated country. According to the Population Reference Bureau, the population was 129.9 million in 2002. With a growth rate of 2.7 percent, the population is expected to double in fewer than twenty-six years.

This nation is young. Approximately 44 percent of Nigerians are younger than fifteen, while only 3 percent are sixty-five or older. In 2002 the annual birthrate was 41 births per 1,000 people, and the death rate was 14 per 1,000. The total fertility rate (the average number of children a woman has in her lifetime) was 5.8.

The greatest population concentrations are in southern cities, such as Lagos and Ibadan, and in the northwest. In contrast, large areas in the northeast are nearly empty. About 64 percent of Nigerians live in rural areas, and the overall population density is 355 people per square mile (140 per sq. km), compared to 24 per square mile (9 per sq. km) in neighboring Niger and 77 per square mile (30 per sq. km) in the United States.

Ethnic Groups and Languages

There are about 250 different ethnic groups in Nigeria, each with its own culture and language. The largest groups are the Hausa, the Fulani, the Yoruba, and the Igbo, which together represent at least 66 percent of the population. Other ethnic groups include the Kanuri, the Ijaw, the Tiv, the Nupe, the Ibibio, the Ogoni, the Ijo, and the Edo.

Northern Nigeria is home to Islamic communities such as the Hausa, the Fulani, and the Kanuri. The primarily Christian Igbo live in the southeast, and the Yoruba, who practice either Christianity or Islam, live in the southwest. The middle belt is the most ethnically complex region of the country, home to more than half of Nigeria's ethnic groups.

Estimates of the number of languages spoken here vary, but there could be as many as 450. English is an official language of the government, and many people use it. French has also been an official language since 1997, but across the country Hausa is the most widely spoken language. Hausa was acquired through exposure to traders

These **Hausa children** are members of Nigeria's largest ethnic group. The Hausa and the Fulani make up about 29 percent of the population.

from across the Sahara, and many words are of Arabic origin. The everyday use of this language is spreading from the Hausa region and is becoming increasingly common in Nigeria's middle belt.

Health

The Nigerian government spends relatively little on health care, and health standards are poor. The nation does not have enough doctors, hospitals, or medications for its citizens. In 1995 there was one doctor for every 3,705 people, one nurse for every 605 people, and one hospital bed for every 1,477 people.

Life expectancy is 52 years for males and 52 for females, slightly higher than West Africa's averages of 50 and 51, respectively. In 2002 the infant mortality rate was 75 for every 1,000 live births. Serious health threats include malnutrition, malaria, and waterborne diseases such as severe diarrhea. Only about half of all Nigerians have access to clean drinking water.

HIV/AIDS One of Nigeria's most pressing health concerns is HIV/AIDS. A report prepared by the Nigerian government and the World Health Organization (WHO) showed that in 2001, 5.8 percent of Nigerian adults, or 3.2 million people, were infected with the HIV virus that causes AIDS. The report predicted that the figure would rise to 4.9 million by 2003.

About 170,000 Nigerians were estimated to have died of AIDS during 2001, and some 1.7 million of the nation's women and 270,000 of its children were living with HIV. Since the crisis began, more than one million Nigerian children have been orphaned because of AIDS. The disease is expected to have a serious long-term impact on families, communities, and economic growth.

The stigma attached to AIDS holds back efforts to prevent its spread. Many people do not admit that they have it, and some claim there is no such disease. During the 1990s, the Abacha government would not allow government health

BOOSTING VACCINATION PROGRAMS

Immunization programs in Nigeria collapsed during the Abacha regime. Only 26 percent of Nigerian children have been vaccinated against measles. International aid organizations reported that a 2001 outbreak of measles afflicted at least 16,000 children in the north. However, the Obasanjo government is putting a greater emphasis on prevention and immunization to prevent future health crises.

ministers to discuss AIDS in public. As a result, many Nigerians have no idea how AIDS is transmitted. Some believe that it is caught from lavatory seats or spread by witchcraft. In fact, the virus is primarily spread through sexual contact. It is difficult, however, to educate people about protecting themselves against this risk because religious leaders and many traditional customs prohibit the frank discussion of sex.

A Nigerian child receives a **checkup and vaccinations.** The government is working to provide better health care.

Swimming in Nigerian rivers can be risky. The biting black fly, which lays its eggs in river water, can transmit parasites that cause river blindness.

Few women practice birth control and men seldom use condoms, increasing the spread of AIDS and other sexually transmitted diseases.

Treatment for AIDS is also minimal in Nigeria. People suffering from the disease often seek cures from traditional healers or Evangelical churches. Such treatments include smearing honey and petroleum jelly on the patient and reading verses of the Koran (the holy text of Islam). To make wider options available, the government announced in 2001 that it would implement a program to provide AIDS medication to thousands of patients. These generic drugs come from India and are a fraction of the cost of drugs produced in Europe or the Americas.

PARASITIC DISEASES Nigerians are also at risk of contracting a number of parasitic diseases common to tropical areas. Malaria is a problem almost everywhere, and children and pregnant women are especially vulnerable. In 1997 there were more than 600,000 cases of this mosquito-borne disease. In 2000 Nigeria was one of several African countries to reduce import taxes on insecticide-treated mosquito nets to make them more affordable.

River blindness, or onchocerciasis, is transmitted by the bite of a black fly. Because the fly lays its eggs in fast-flowing water, people living near rivers are at the highest risk. The fly's bite releases microscopic worms into the body that make the skin itchy and can cause blindness. A safe and effective treatment became available in the 1980s, and river blindness has been brought under control in much of West Africa. Nigeria was late in adopting a treatment program, however, and the disease is still present.

Guinea worm is another debilitating disease in Nigeria's rural areas. It is contracted by drinking water contaminated with larvae. Inside the human body, the worms mature, growing up to 3 to 5 feet long (0.9 to 1.5 m) in one year. After the worms mate, the females migrate under the skin and gradually work their way out of the body, causing terrible pain and illness.

Efforts to eradicate guinea worm, such as using cloth filters to strain out the larvae, are making progress. According to the United Nations Children's Fund (UNICEF), cases dropped from 394,000 in 1990 to fewer than 7,900 in 2000. However, authorities in many poor communities still need to improve water supplies by digging underground wells or by chemically treating the water.

Other parasitic diseases still problematic in Nigeria are schistosomiasis, or snail fever, a treatable disease that is contracted by bathing in contaminated water, and elephantiasis, or lymphatic filariasis, in which worms transmitted by mosquitoes block the lymph system. Nigeria has the second highest number of people infected with elephantiasis in the world after India, but medication is expected to bring this disease under control by 2015.

Underground wells prevent the spread of guinea worm disease. Well water is closed off from the open air and is less likely to be contaminated by the worms than open water.

Nigeria's best educated and most ambitious people are its greatest resource. But many of them have left the country, at least for a while. Among the millions of Nigerians who live abroad are physicians, lawyers, bankers, and other skilled professionals. Some have returned to their homeland since the democratic government took office in 1999.

Education

Nigeria has a long way to go in providing its people with good education. The national rate of adult illiteracy in 2000 was 27.7 percent for men and 43.8 percent for women, according to estimates by the United Nations Educational, Scientific, and Cultural Organization (UNESCO).

Nigeria's state and federal governments share responsibility for education, and there are also a large number of privately owned schools. Public education is free and compulsory for every child aged six to fifteen. Children attend primary school for six years, junior secondary school for three years, and senior secondary school for another three. Schools put an emphasis on science. The federal government also runs technical/vocational colleges, teacher-training colleges, and universities throughout the country.

In 1994 some 16.2 million Nigerian children were enrolled in primary schools, dropping to 4.6 million students enrolled in secondary schools. While nearly 100 percent of boys attended primary school, only 87 percent of

A teacher and students focus on the day's lesson. Educated women are vital to the success of teaching the next generations of Nigerians.

girls did so, and at the secondary level enrollment fell to 36 percent of boys and 30 percent of girls.

Women's Rights

Women's situations vary among different ethnic groups and regions in Nigeria. In the Islamic north, where people follow strict Sharia laws, most women stay at home, and only the daughters of elite families attend secondary school. Women in the south are more likely to be educated.

Many Yoruba women achieve some degree of independence because their traditional role involves selling goods at the market. However, a bank won't give a woman a loan without a letter of guarantee from her husband, and some traditions prohibit women from inheriting property.

In some Nigerian communities a woman is considered to belong to her husband's family since his family paid a bride price to hers when they married. Polygyny, or the practice of men having multiple wives, is common. Some women do not like the custom, while others find that it gives them more freedom to engage in activities such as trading at the market while another wife looks after the household.

In 2001 Human Rights Watch, an international human rights organization, reported that women's rights in Nigeria are often violated. For example, it is not a crime for a man to rape or to beat his wife, if traditional law allows this, unless she is seriously injured. International trafficking (selling) of women is also a problem. The trafficked women

are often sent to other West African countries or to Europe and forced into prostitution. Child marriages are common, especially in the north, as is child labor (usually unpaid domestic work).

Few women have ever been elected to public office, although the current government has appointed some women to government positions. Nigerian women complain that men put many obstacles in the way to prevent them from running for office or pursuing other goals. Women are traditionally thought of as merely someone's daughter, wife, sister, or widow, and this perception limits their opportunities. Nevertheless, many modern Nigerian women have obtained university degrees and have achieved professional success.

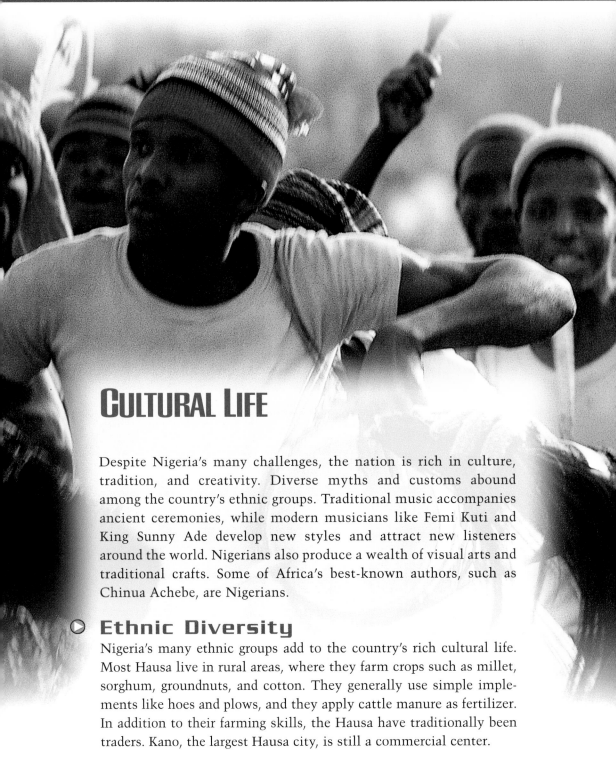

CULTURAL LIFE

Despite Nigeria's many challenges, the nation is rich in culture, tradition, and creativity. Diverse myths and customs abound among the country's ethnic groups. Traditional music accompanies ancient ceremonies, while modern musicians like Femi Kuti and King Sunny Ade develop new styles and attract new listeners around the world. Nigerians also produce a wealth of visual arts and traditional crafts. Some of Africa's best-known authors, such as Chinua Achebe, are Nigerians.

◗ Ethnic Diversity

Nigeria's many ethnic groups add to the country's rich cultural life. Most Hausa live in rural areas, where they farm crops such as millet, sorghum, groundnuts, and cotton. They generally use simple implements like hoes and plows, and they apply cattle manure as fertilizer. In addition to their farming skills, the Hausa have traditionally been traders. Kano, the largest Hausa city, is still a commercial center.

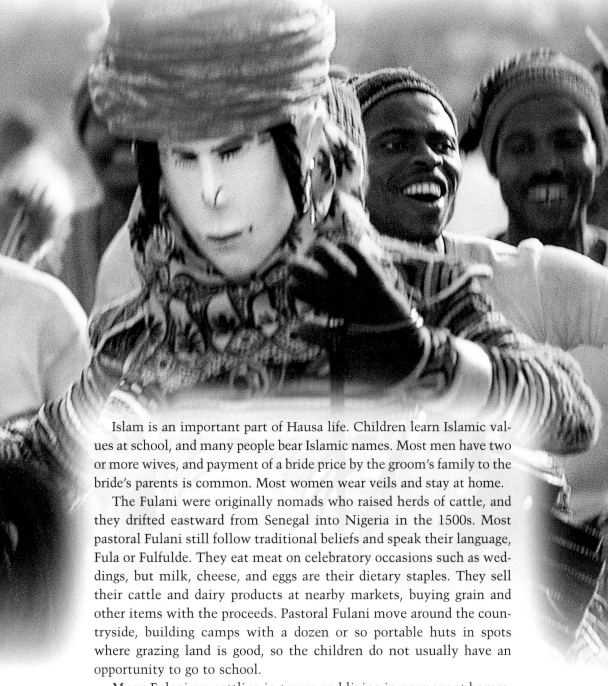

Islam is an important part of Hausa life. Children learn Islamic values at school, and many people bear Islamic names. Most men have two or more wives, and payment of a bride price by the groom's family to the bride's parents is common. Most women wear veils and stay at home.

The Fulani were originally nomads who raised herds of cattle, and they drifted eastward from Senegal into Nigeria in the 1500s. Most pastoral Fulani still follow traditional beliefs and speak their language, Fula or Fulfulde. They eat meat on celebratory occasions such as weddings, but milk, cheese, and eggs are their dietary staples. They sell their cattle and dairy products at nearby markets, buying grain and other items with the proceeds. Pastoral Fulani move around the countryside, building camps with a dozen or so portable huts in spots where grazing land is good, so the children do not usually have an opportunity to go to school.

Many Fulani are settling in towns and living in permanent homes. Most of these Fulani are devout Muslims who follow Sharia laws.

Yoruba men walk past the **Central Mosque** in downtown Lagos. Many Yoruba live in cities and practice the Islamic religion. To learn more about the Yoruba and other Nigerian cultures, go to vgsbooks.com.

Many have adopted the Hausa language and culture, intermarried with Hausa families, and formed the upper class of their communities. Many Fulani children have often been well educated in Islamic beliefs and have also received Western-style education.

Many Yoruba are city dwellers and make up a majority of the population of Lagos and Ibadan. The Yoruba speak a common language, although there are a variety of local dialects. Religion creates another common bond among the Yoruba. Many individuals who are officially Christian or Muslim combine these faiths with aspects of traditional religion, worshipping a supreme creator and hundreds of lesser gods. Many Yoruba consult oracles and turn to traditional religion when faced with difficulties or illness.

The average Yoruba family extends to include distant relatives, and marriage is viewed as a union of the two extended families, not just the married couple. Marriage can be monogamous or polygynous, and divorce is frowned upon. Young people treat Yoruba elders with great respect.

Within Igbo communities, people make their mark by accumulating wealth, a good education, and political influence. They value personal achievement, but many other Nigerians, who attach more importance to the community than to the individual, resent this and think of the Igbo as pushy or aggressive.

Igbo families may be monogamous or polygynous. Since the Igbo think of a wife as the property of her husband's family, a widow may marry her husband's brother. Families value children highly, and Igbo men tend to blame a woman who does not bear children, especially males, for this result. A naming ceremony is held for each baby, and every Igbo name has a special meaning relating to an ancestor or an event, or, if the family is Christian, referring to God. Most Igbo are Christian, but many also worship the gods of their ancestors and consult sacred oracles to solve problems or to resolve disputes.

Religion

About 48 percent of Nigerians are Muslim, 34 percent follow Christianity, and 18 percent follow other beliefs, including traditional African religions. Most Nigerian Muslims are Sunni (a branch of Islam). Islam has had followers in the region since about A.D. 1100, and Christianity was introduced later by European missionaries. Roman Catholic, Anglican, Methodist, and Baptist Christian faiths are widely practiced. Pentecostal Christianity attracts many followers in the south, and one church near Lagos can seat more than fifty thousand people.

The widespread African practice of polygyny is accepted in Islamic families, but the Christian churches do not condone it. Many Nigerians follow traditional religious practices as well as Islam or Christianity, and the spirits and gods of the ancestors and of nature seldom seem far away. Nigerian traditional religions usually have a supreme being and numerous lesser deities, or gods and goddesses.

Nigerians dance a **spiritual trance dance.** Others attend a **Christian service.** Nigerian spirituality is often a blend of traditional religion and ideas from Christianity or Islam.

The **Argungu Fishing Festival** occurs over several days each February and March. Hundreds of men and boys plunge into the Sokoto River in a frenzy to net the biggest fish.

Messengers between gods and humans include major and minor deities, ancestors, folk heroes, and spirits that inhabit the hills, forests, and waters. People hold rituals and festivals, build shrines, and observe taboos to ensure that these intermediaries are friendly.

Holidays and Festivals

Every ethnic group has its own traditional festivals to honor the gods, the ancestors, or the spirits who protect the community. Egungun, when people honor the spirits of their ancestors by dancing in masks and costumes, is the biggest annual Yoruba festival. Just before the yam harvest begins, the Igbo celebrate the Festival of the New Yam to honor the earth goddess and ensure a good harvest. This is a time to clean, scrub, and start fresh. Wrestling matches and feasts also take place.

The town of Argungu is famed for its annual fishing festival in early spring. Hundreds of men jump into the Sokoto River with their nets to try to catch huge perch. Canoe and swimming races are also held.

Muslims also take part in durbar festivals at least twice each year. These traditional celebrations are held on Mouloud (Birth of the Prophet) and on Eid al-Fitr. Eid al-Fitr is a feastday marking the end of Ramadan, the Islamic month of fasting. After prayers are said at durbars, area chiefs—accompanied by singers, musicians, and men on charging horses—join in a procession to the local emir's palace. Sometimes special durbars are held to observe nonreligious occasions. For example, a huge durbar was held when Nigeria became independent in 1960.

Nigeria's national holiday celebrating independence from colonial rule is observed every October 1. Other public holidays include New Year's Day on January 1 and Christmas on December 25 and 26. Easter is celebrated over four days in the spring. Islamic holidays celebrated as national holidays are dependent on the Islamic lunar calendar and vary from year to year. They include Eid al-Kabir (the Feast of the Sacrifice), Eid al-Fitr, and Mouloud.

● Food

Food is an important part of Nigerian life. Local cooks prepare favorite dishes for special occasions. The Festival of the New Yam features treats made of the celebrated vegetable, and fish dishes abound at the Argungu festival. Other events, such as the naming of a Yoruba baby, have their own food customs.

For everyday fare, the staples of the Nigerian diet include cassavas, yams, and rice. The nation's rich abundance of fruits also adds color and flavor the meals. Beer and palm wine are popular adult drinks.

Most Nigerians eat their main meals in the afternoon or evening. *Fufu* (also spelled *foufou* or *foo-foo*), a starchy snack made with cassava, yam, and plantain (a relative of the banana), accompanies many meals. Soup is popular at midday. The Yoruba enjoy *egusi* soup.

CRACKING THE KOLA NUT

The kola nut is more than just a bitter-tasting nut. It is used as a symbolic food in several Nigerian cultures. Breaking open the kola nut is an Igbo ritual for welcoming visitors. The Yoruba use the kola nut in rituals to foresee success or avoid failure. The Yoruba also use the nut in naming ceremonies, in which it symbolizes longevity and wisdom.

Egusi is made with ground melon seeds, meat, shrimp, and hot chili peppers. Other favorites include fish pepper soup and groundnut soup. *Ikokore,* made with fish and ground yams, is popular in western Nigeria, and so is *jollof* rice. This hearty dish consists of rice with vegetables and meat or fish. *Ukwaka* is a steamed pudding made with corn and plantains.

In addition to main meals, Nigerians love to snack. Popular snack foods include fried yam chips, fried plantains, and boiled groundnuts. Other treats are *kulikuli* (fried peanut paste) and *suya* (spicy meat kabobs).

PEPPER SOUP

Nigerian recipes are often very spicy, so use smaller quantities of spices if you prefer a milder soup. In Nigeria, this popular dish would probably be made with goat meat, but if that is hard to find, use beef or chicken. The dish is usually served with rice.

2 tablespoons cooking oil (use palm oil for a more authentic taste, if you can find it)

2 onions, chopped

2 or 3 pounds stewing beef or chicken, cut into bite-sized pieces

about 1 cup water

3 or 4 fresh tomatoes, chopped or put through a blender, or a 6-ounce can tomato paste plus a 16-ounce can tomato sauce

1 or 2 green bell peppers

1 teaspoon dried red pepper, crushed or ground, or 2 or 3 hot chili peppers, cleaned and chopped

2 beef or vegetable bouillon cubes

1 teaspoon curry powder

salt and black pepper to taste

1. Heat the oil in a stewing pot over medium heat. Add onions and sauté until tender.
2. Add meat to the pot, with just enough water to cover the meat. Adjust heat to high, and boil until meat starts to get tender. Lower heat to medium.
3. If you are using fresh tomatoes, chop them or put them through the blender. Chop or blend green peppers.
4. Add tomatoes or tomato paste and sauce and green peppers to pot. Add bouillon cubes and spices. Return mixture to a boil for a minute or two. Reduce heat and simmer for about half an hour, stirring occasionally. Serve hot.

Serves 6 to 8.

This young Igbo girl stands proudly beside an elaborate **Enugu masquerade headdress.**

Visual Arts and Crafts

Traditional West African art includes both functional and purely decorative objects, but artworks are seldom personal or emotional statements. Instead, sculptures, masks, jewelry, music, and dance are closely tied to religious beliefs and community activities.

For example, works of art play a role in the ceremonies of many religious cults. Yoruba cults are dedicated to deities such as Shango, the god of thunder, and Ifa, the god of knowledge. Cult followers use a variety of objects in their rituals. These objects include memorial beads, mud figures, masks, and sculptures of ancestors kept in shrines. The Ijo people of the delta use masks in the form of aquatic animals such as the hippopotamus and the crocodile in activities related to the cults of water spirits.

Elaborate masks and costumes are used in masquerade performances held to mark a variety of circumstances, including initiation ceremonies and sacred rituals. Often these performances carry social messages, with characters behaving in appropriate and inappropriate manners. Characters portrayed in Ijo masquerades, for example, include a miser, a greedy person, and an unscrupulous person. The Igbo and Ibibio make masks with distorted or asymmetrical features to represent evil or dangerous figures in their masquerade performances. Northern Igbo make spectacular 12-foot-high (3.7-m) tiered masks to honor the dead and to ensure the community's future well-being.

Most African art follows symbolic or abstract designs, and the emphasis is on overall resemblance rather than exact representation. In Yoruba art, a straight, smooth shape denotes youth and good health, and symmetry is desirable even if it means a pose appears unnatural.

Benin bronze head

Nigerian art is most famous for its ancient masterpieces. Nok artists sculpted expressive terra-cotta heads around 500 B.C., and the realistic bronze and terra-cotta portraits from Ife date to about the ninth century A.D. The Benin Bronzes, a collection of detailed bronze figures and plaques from the Kingdom of Benin, have also assured the country's importance in art history.

In the 1960s, an artistic community was established at Oshogbo, and artists trained there experimented with new techniques applied to traditional subjects. Several, such as artists Taiwo Olaniyi (also known as Twins Seven Seven) and Jimoh Buraimoh, continue to be very successful.

Nigeria also maintains a strong tradition of crafts and handiwork, creating leatherwork, textiles, pottery, and decorative calabashes. Calabashes are dried gourds that are cleaned out and decorated and used as rafts, musical instruments, or food containers.

The Nupe are skilled in embroidery, weaving, and bead making. They also make carved wooden doors and carved and painted masks. The Hausa are known for their leather saddles, sheaths, and bags, as well as for weavings, gold and silver jewelry, and embroidery. In some cultures, the human body itself is an object to be decorated with elaborate hair sculptures or body scarring. The nomadic Fulani are famous for their body decorations, as well as for the engraved gourds that they use for carrying milk.

Architecture

A wide range of building styles—from mud-walled granaries (storehouses for grain), mosques, and royal palaces to modern office buildings—can be seen in this diverse country. In traditional Igbo villages, homes are designed as family compounds. Rather than sharing one big house per family, the head of

Traditional Igbo dwelling and compound

the household and each of his wives with her children have their own small dwellings. The Yoruba build their homes around courtyards where family members get together to work and chat. During European exploration and colonization, two- or three-story single-family houses were introduced to the region and became symbols of status and modern life.

Nigerians like to decorate the exteriors of their homes. Hausa homes are decorated inside and out with molded and painted decorations, primarily geometric patterns,

Decorated Hausa home

although some people include the shapes of bicycles, cars, or clocks in their designs. Traditional Yoruba houses had carved doors, and decorated posts supported the veranda.

Building materials and designs vary according to local conditions. In the north, homes have stone foundations to discourage termites. People around Nok build oval mud-walled houses with thatched roofs and a grain storage area integrated into the back of the house.

Theater, Literature, and Music

Nigerian culture has a long tradition of oral storytelling, legends, recitations, and songs. Contemporary live theater started with dramatizations of Bible stories in the 1940s. New plays based on African themes were written following independence, especially satires on political, religious, and social themes. In addition to live drama, Nigerians enjoy television shows and comedies. The local film industry is very small, but movies from the United States and India are popular with audiences.

Nigeria has produced a number of authors who are recognized and admired around the world. The first to make a mark in literary circles was Chinua Achebe with his novel *Things Fall Apart*. In 1986 Wole Soyinka became the first African to win the Nobel Prize for literature. Other well-known Nigerian writers include Buchi Emecheta, Flora Nwapa, and Ben Okri, winner of the 1991 Booker Prize for his novel *The Famished Road*.

THINGS FALL APART

Things Fall Apart, by Chinua Achebe, is one of the best-known novels ever written about Africa. First published in 1958, it has been studied by students in Africa and around the world ever since. It is the story of a proud Igbo wrestler, his wives, and his fellow villagers. Their way of life is destroyed when Christian missionaries and colonial administrators arrive.

Like storytelling, music and dance are more than entertainment in Africa. They bring communities together and are central to every festival and special occasion. Sometimes everyone dances. At other times, only trained dancers may perform certain dances.

Traditional music is heard at Nigerian social occasions. These may include weddings and funerals, during religious ceremonies, to announce the beginning of a festival, and to announce the arrival of a visitor to a royal palace. Drums of various shapes and sizes are the most popular African instrument, and drummers play complex rhythms as several variations of the beat weave in and out simultaneously. Bells, rattles, xylophones, and wind instruments such as flutes, horns, and trumpets are also played. Stringed instruments

Traveling theater performers dance and act out a play in a Nigerian village. Storytelling, acting, and dance have long been an important part of traditional Nigerian culture.

In the past, **Yoruba drummers** played to call and speak to the spirits. In modern Nigeria, their sound also accompanies traditional and pop music.

such as the *goje,* a single-stringed fiddle, are made with hair, twisted hide, or metal cords stretched across a sound box made of wood or a calabash. Instruments are often elaborately decorated.

Nigeria has several recording studios, and the local contemporary music industry has produced some famous stars. Although there is a huge market for music at home, Nigerian entertainers are not well known outside Africa. The late Fela Kuti developed and popularized Afro-beat music, a blend of African music, jazz, and soul. Fela's son, Femi Kuti, has his own successful music career. In the 1920s, a new style called *juju* music appeared. Juju features vocal harmonies and guitar backed by traditional drums, and it remains very popular. King Sunny Ade is the best-known juju music performer. The Nigerian-born pop singer Sade Adu also has a large following around the world.

The Yoruba can make their drums talk. Cords that vary the tension on the drum's surface allow the instrument to produce different notes. Skilled drummers vary the pitch and rhythm to imitate the tones of language. Talking drums are used for sending messages, for dances, and for reciting traditional proverbs.

Dambe, a form of boxing, originated with the Hausa people. During a dambe match, two boxers fought for the honor of their villages. The sport remains popular in Nigeria and is gaining international attention.

Games and Sports

One of the most popular traditional games in African nations is *ayo,* known outside of Nigeria as *mancala.* Ayo is a strategic board game in which players move pebbles, seeds, or other markers in a series of holes in a piece of wood or in the ground. The object is to capture more markers than one's opponent as the game proceeds.

For fun, boys spin snail shells like tops. Girls like to match an opponent's steps and hops while friends clap and sing. Another popular game involves tossing a pebble in the air and scooping up lots of pebbles from the ground with the same hand. Still another game challenges people to balance objects on their outstretched legs. Players try to pass the objects, using only their legs, without dropping them.

Wrestling is a traditional Nigerian sport that serves as entertainment, as a means of settling quarrels, and as a way to test young men for bravery and resourcefulness. Singing and dancing accompany traditional wrestling matches. A form of boxing known as *dambe* is popular in northern states. Opponents can hit with only one cloth-wrapped hand, although kicking is also permitted.

People in northern Nigeria enjoy racing camels and horses, while boat and canoe races are common in the delta. Wealthy Nigerians like rugby, polo, golf, tennis, and cricket, the latter introduced by the British. The British also introduced soccer (known in Nigeria as football), and it remains a national passion. The country's greatest soccer moment came when the men's national team won a gold medal at the 1996 Summer Olympics.

Nigeria has taken part in international sporting competitions since the early 1950s, winning its first gold medal in the high jump at the Commonwealth Games in 1954. Nigerian boxers have been particularly successful at the Olympics, the Commonwealth Games, and other international events. Famous athletes include sprinter Mary Onyali, soccer star Rasheed Yekini, and National Basketball Association (NBA) player Hakeem Olajuwon.

Nigerian football fans avidly follow the ups and downs of the national men's team, the Super Eagles, as they compete against other African teams and in world meets. The women's squad, the Super Falcons, is one of the best women's teams in Africa.

Taribo West *(right)* of the **Nigerian Super Eagles** goes toe to toe with Argentine player Ariel Ortega during the 1996 Summer Olympics. The Nigerian national team took the match, winning the gold medal in soccer.

THE ECONOMY

Nigeria is rich in resources, but its people are extremely poor. The gross national product (GNP)—the value of goods and services produced annually by the country's citizens—is about $36 million, or $300 per capita. According to the World Bank, approximately 70 percent of the population live on about $1 a day. A combination of government inefficiency and corruption, unreliable services, and outbreaks of ethnic and religious violence have all contributed to a stagnant economy.

A heavy dependence on oil revenues has also contributed to economic instability. Petroleum brought in 97.6 percent of Nigeria's export earnings in 1997. This reliance on only one resource is a problem, especially since the oil industry creates relatively few jobs. Once the oil has been found and export facilities built, few workers are needed. The government has made huge sums from oil revenues, and some of this money has been stolen from the government or spent on extravagant projects. Meanwhile, not enough has been invested in the community to create new jobs.

◯ Industry and Trade

Industry, including mining, manufacturing, construction, and power, employs about 6 percent of the employed labor force. Industry contributed an estimated 33.5 percent of the gross domestic product (GDP)—the value of production within the country's borders by citizens and noncitizens—in 1998. Mining represents 27.2 percent of the GDP. Nigeria operates tin and iron-ore mines. It is also Africa's biggest petroleum-producing nation, able to deliver up to 2 million barrels per day. For many years, most of the natural gas associated with oil reserves was wastefully burned off. Exports of liquefied natural gas, which began in 1999, have helped to reduce this practice. A natural gas pipeline is planned to supply natural gas to nearby Benin, Togo, and Ghana.

A number of international oil companies operate in the delta. Royal Dutch/Shell is the largest, accounting for just under half of the country's oil production. Others include ChevronTexaco Corporation and ExxonMobil. These and other companies plan to invest billions of dollars.

Commuters wait in a **gas line.**

FINDING FUEL

Despite Nigeria's wealth of oil, Nigerians have to deal with constant fuel shortages. People must line up, sometimes for hours, to buy gas. The refineries that convert the oil to usable fuel products have not been maintained and only produce a third of the gasoline they should. So one of the world's major oil-producing countries spends billions of naira to subsidize imported fuel. Another cause of the shortages is that, because of low fuel prices in Nigeria, people smuggle it to neighboring countries where it fetches a higher price. In 2002 the government began to raise the price of fuel and made plans to transfer the industry from public to private ownership.

The funds will develop gas resources and new technologies and will continue exploration of deep underground oil fields. Oil refineries and petrochemical industries are located in several cities, including Kaduna and Warri.

Manufacturing represented 5.4 percent of the GDP in 1998, and employed 4.3 percent of the country's workers in 1986. Major manufacturing activities include food processing (especially palm oil), brewing, iron and steel, motor vehicle assembly from imported parts, textiles, cigarettes, footwear, pulp and paper, and cement.

Principal exports from Nigeria include oil, cocoa, and rubber. The main imports are machinery and transportation equipment, chemicals, food, and other manufactured goods. The United States is Nigeria's major export market—it buys much of its oil—but Germany, Spain, Italy, and France are also important customers. Import suppliers include Britain, the United States, Germany, France, and Japan. Nigeria does not have strong trade ties with other African nations. The bulk of domestically traded goods—primarily agricultural products—

move between the north and the south and between the heavily populated cities of the southeast and the southwest.

The services sector contributed almost 27 percent of GDP in 1997 and employed 48.5 percent of the workers in 1986. This sector includes government employees, teachers, and hotel and restaurant staff. Nigeria has few tourists because of its reputation for being a difficult and dangerous destination. Most visitors come from neighboring African countries like Niger and Benin, but some come from Europe.

There is also a huge underground economy. It doesn't show up in official statistics, but various estimates put its value at between 40 and 77 percent of GDP. This "invisible" economy is where many Nigerians, especially young people, find employment. They may work as minibus drivers or as traders in the markets where people buy their groceries. The underground economy, sometimes referred to as the shadow or black market economy, is unregulated and untaxed, but it is essential to everyday life.

Agriculture

Agriculture (including hunting, forestry, and fishing) is a mainstay of the Nigerian economy. It made up an estimated 39 percent of GDP in 1998 and employed 34.2 percent of the labor force in 1999.

Most Nigerian farmers use traditional, rather than mechanized, methods of farming. Different regions produce different crops. Root crops, including yams and cassavas, thrive in the middle belt.

Much of Nigeria's agriculture remains traditional rather than mechanical. This traditional farmer is **handpicking yams.**

Nigerian farmers usually plant **rice** from April to May and harvest it between August and November.

Fruits, vegetables, and cereals such as maize, wheat, rice, millet, and guinea corn can be grown in both the north and the south. Cotton, coffee, and sugarcane come predominantly from the north, while kola nuts, cocoa, palms, and rubber trees thrive in the south.

The major food crops are yams, cassavas, maize, millet, rice, and beans. Cocoa, palm kernels, cotton, and rubber are other important products. Before Nigeria became independent, agricultural goods, particularly cocoa, rubber, and palm oil, made up most of the country's export earnings, and the nation was also one of the world's leading producers of groundnuts. In the twenty-first century, most of Nigeria's agricultural products are sold locally rather than exported.

Southern Nigeria has little livestock because of the presence of the tsetse fly, which carries the parasitic infection trypanosomiasis. Also called sleeping sickness, some strains of the disease are fatal to livestock, while others can be transmitted by the tsetse fly to humans. The Sudan Savanna in the north is valuable for cattle rearing because of the relative absence of the fly. Cattle, sheep, and goats are raised to produce milk, meat, and leather, and people also raise chickens and ducks.

Nigerians fish for freshwater fish from small boats in Lake Chad. They catch several species of catfish in the country's rivers and streams.

Trawlers bring in saltwater fish species, shrimp, and other crustaceans along the coast. Some Nigerians are employed in aquaculture, or fish farming.

Transportation, Energy, and Communication

There are many ways to get around in Nigeria, although roads and port facilities have not been well maintained. Most Nigerians travel by road, either by car, bus, or bush taxi (a vehicle similar to a van). The nation has an extensive network of roads, covering more than 120,000 miles (193,116 km), including some 700 miles (1,127 km) of multilane highways. The country has one of Africa's largest rail systems, with 2,177 miles (3,503 km) of tracks linking southern ports with the north. The railway system is operated by the state-owned Nigeria Railway Corporation. The main international airport is in Lagos, but there are also large airports in Port Harcourt, Kano, and Abuja. The main air carrier is Nigeria Airways, a state-owned company that the government is working to transfer to private control.

The Niger River is navigable by riverboat and barge as far as Lokoja. Ports farther upstream are accessible during the high water season. Lagos is the main port, handling about three-quarters of the cargo

Roadwork is a welcome sight to Nigerians. Most of Nigeria's people travel by motor vehicle, but the nation has a reputation for bad roadways.

Once the main method of transportation, **riverboats** are still common on Nigeria's large rivers.

arriving and leaving the country. Other ports include Port Harcourt, Calabar, and Warri.

Like transportation facilities, the water and energy sources needed for economic development have been neglected in Nigeria. Some hotels truck and treat their own water, and most businesses own diesel generators because the state-run power supply is so erratic. Most power comes from thermal plants that use domestic oil, natural gas, or coal, but they became run-down, and at times they have only been able to produce a quarter of their capacity. Repairs are bringing them back on-line, but they are not yet able to meet energy demands. Only about 40 percent of homes in Nigeria are connected to the state power system.

Phone service is also unreliable, and fewer than 1 in 250 Nigerian households is connected to phone lines. Mobile telephone service became available in 2001. With a huge potential market, mobile phone shops immediately sprang up. Although service is too expensive for most ordinary citizens, some people share phones to cut costs. Many Nigerians can access the Internet relatively inexpensively at cyber cafés in towns and cities.

The electricity supply in Nigeria is so unreliable that people joke that NEPA, the acronym for the National Electric Power Authority, the state-owned electricity company, really stands for "Never Expect Power Always" or "Never Electric Power Always."

The media is a thriving sector of Nigeria's communication industry, although it has struggled in the past. The nation has a tradition of freedom of the press, but military dictators have sometimes restricted that freedom. Nevertheless, the country has almost eighty national and local newspapers and many magazines, most of them privately owned. In 1996 twenty-five of these publications were dailies, with a combined circulation of 2.7 million. Electronic media outlets are primarily state owned, and there are about fifty television stations and forty radio stations.

Overcoming Corruption

Nigeria has a well-educated elite and much economic potential, with water, arable land, and natural resources. Its people have a reputation for being creative, energetic, and resilient, but there is also a legacy of violence and corruption. Despite its rich resources, the majority of the people remain poor. Between 1979, when Obasanjo last ran the country, and 1999, when he was elected president, the economy had slipped backward, and per capita annual income had fallen. When Obasanjo took power, Nigerians were optimistic about change. After three years of democracy, however, people were becoming impatient and complained that political freedom had not brought improved living standards.

The government plans to sell many of the businesses it owns to the private sector, a move many hope will increase competition, attract new investment, and improve services to the public. Other initiatives—such as plans to buy new government jets and to build an expensive national soccer stadium—frustrate Nigerians. The country is more than $30 billion in debt and and has not fully funded education and healthcare.

Workers for a government **building project** construct a new clinic. Many Nigerians are frustrated that more government funds do not go toward health care and community development.

HUMAN RIGHTS PANEL

Among those who appeared before the human rights panel was President Obasanjo. He appeared once as a plaintiff to testify about his imprisonment between 1995 and 1996. He appeared a second time because he was accused of ordering an army raid on the home of musician Fela Kuti that resulted in the death of the singer's mother several months later. Former presidents Muhammad Buhari, Ibrahim Babangida, and Abdulsalami Abubakar refused orders to appear. Buhari was to be questioned about how a former government minister came to be bound, drugged, and placed in a crate. Babangida was accused of involvement in the killing of a journalist. Abubakar was called to answer questions about the death of Abiola.

The Nigerian government's image continues to suffer as a result of widespread corruption, and many people do not trust their leaders. A nongovernmental watchdog organization named Nigeria the world's second most corrupt country after Bangladesh in 2001. Some of the country's richest citizens are former generals or politicians. Contracts to supply goods or services to the government often go to companies with connections to the people who hand out the contracts. Nigerians routinely have to pay bribes to receive their passports or to get telephones installed. Some people blame corruption on poor leadership, while others say that all Nigerians have to be accountable for their actions before change will occur.

Nigeria is also trying to come to terms with its human rights record. Obasanjo's government set up a Human Rights Violations Investigation Commission to look into abuses alleged to have been committed between 1966 and 1999. Modeled partly on South Africa's Truth  and Reconciliation Commission, the panel investigated cases of alleged torture and murder. It wrapped up its hearings in October 2001. In 2002 the panel made recommendations for reform, and Nigerians are watching the developments closely.

◎ The Future

Like most developing countries, Nigeria is a mix of traditional cultures and European and American ideas. To find the best solutions for Nigeria, its leaders must reconcile these different influences. Democracy and the self-rule of a state that was arbitrarily created by foreigners are some of the ideas to which the country must adapt.

After almost thirty years of military rule, Nigerians have returned to democracy. However, they have little faith in their government, and many see it as an organization that victimizes rather than serves them. They tend to identify more with their ethnic group than with the nation, leading some observers to worry that the country will split apart along ethnic lines.

Nigeria continues to struggle with other internal troubles. More than six thousand people were killed in religious and ethnic conflicts between 1999 and 2001. The year 2001 also brought deadly outbreaks of infectious diseases and the shooting death of the country's minister of justice. In 2002 an explosion in a Lagos army munitions depot left more than one thousand people dead. Meanwhile, some Nigerians complained that the government seemed unable to end the violence, while others—fearing the return of military government—were concerned by Obasanjo's dependence on the army to restore order. Others watched preparations for the 2003 presidential and parliamentary elections, which were already the subject of rumors of corruption.

In addition to encouraging democracy within the country, Nigeria's government is also trying to foster it in other African nations. President Obasanjo is one of several African leaders, including the presidents of South Africa, Algeria, and Senegal, who have created NEPAD (New Partnership for Africa's Development). The program's goal is to bring increased investment, trade, and aid to African countries that make democratic reforms.

Many people in Nigeria and around the world hope that this nation's democratic government will succeed. With political unrest in surrounding countries, a strong democracy in Nigeria would help stabilize the region. A strong economy would have far-reaching benefits. A lot is at stake as the giant of Africa faces the future.

Federal buildings such as this one are a symbol of corruption to many Nigerians. Leaders are striving to regain the people's trust.

Timeline

CA. 9000 B.C.   Evidence of early human inhabitants exists in Nigeria.

CA. 500 B.C.   The Nok culture, known for terra-cotta figurines, arises in central Nigeria.

CA. 450 B.C.   Iron-smelting furnaces are used in Nigeria.

CA. A.D. 1100   Islamic merchants from North Africa introduce their religion to northern Nigeria.

CA. 1400s   Kingdom of Benin grows into a powerful city-state.

CA. 1480s   The Atlantic slave trade increases rapidly.

1481   Portuguese representatives visit the oba of Benin.

CA. 1500–1591   The Songhai Empire dominates northwestern Nigeria.

CA. 1591–1790   The Bornu Empire takes power in the north.

1804   The Sokoto jihad begins.

1807   Britain votes to abolish the Atlantic slave trade.

1817   The first Yoruba civil wars begin.

CA. 1860   The Atlantic slave trade ends.

1861   The British annex Lagos.

1879   The United Africa Company (later the Royal Niger Company) is founded.

1884–1885   The Berlin West Africa Conference takes place, during which European powers agree on the division of Africa.

1886   The Yoruba civil wars end.

1897   The British conquer the Kingdom of Benin.

1903   Britain establishes the protectorates of Northern and Southern Nigeria.

1903   Frederick Lugard leads attacks on Kano and Sokoto.

1914   Nigeria becomes a British colony. World War I begins.

1923   Nigeria's first political party is formed.

1930s   The anticolonial movement begins in Nigeria.

1939–1945   World War II

1958   Chinua Achebe's *Things Fall Apart* is published. The first shipment of Nigerian oil is exported.

1960   Nigeria achieves independence.

1967-1970   The Biafran civil war

1979   Olusegun Obasanjo hands over government to civilian rule.

1985   A military coup brings General Ibrahim Babangida to power amid a crash in oil prices.

1986   Wole Soyinka becomes the first African to receive the Nobel Prize for literature.

1991   The nation's capital officially moves from Lagos to Abuja.

1993   Chief Moshood Abiola wins the majority of votes in a popular election. The election is annulled, and General Sani Abacha seizes power.

1995   Activist Ken Saro-Wiwa is executed. Nigeria is suspended from the Commonwealth.

1996   Nigeria wins the gold medal in soccer at the Summer Olympics.

1997   Afro-beat musician Fela Kuti dies of AIDS.

1999   Olusegun Obasanjo is elected president.

2000   Clashes between Muslims and Christians in Kaduna state leave at least two thousand people dead.

2001   A dozen states have implemented or announced that they plan to implement Sharia either in full or in part.

2002   Deadly clashes between Nigerian Muslims and Christians are sparked by the 2002 Miss World Pageant. Scheduled to be held in Abuja, the pageant is moved to London, England, after more than two hundred people are killed in the renewed religious violence.

COUNTRY NAME Federal Republic of Nigeria

AREA 356,669 square miles (931,543 sq. km)

MAIN LANDFORMS Northern High Plains, Jos Plateau, Eastern Highlands, Niger-Benue River Valley, Niger Delta

HIGHEST POINT Dimlang Peak, 6,699 feet (2,042 m) above sea level

LOWEST POINT Sea level

MAJOR RIVERS Niger River, Benue River, Kaduna River

ANIMALS Roan antelopes, gorillas, hairy mangrove crabs, Nile crocodiles, hornbills, guinea fowl, giraffes, pygmy hippos.

CAPITAL CITY Abuja

OTHER MAJOR CITIES Lagos, Ibadan, Kano

OFFICIAL LANGUAGES English and French

MONETARY UNIT Naira. 1 naira = 100 kobo

NIGERIAN CURRENCY

In 1959 the Central Bank of Nigeria was established, and Nigerian currency was introduced. The naira was equal to the British pound. In 1973 the naira was converted to a decimal currency, with 100 kobo equal to 1 naira. The Nigerian Security Printing and Minting Company (NSPMC) issues bills in denominations starting at 5 naira, and a new 500-naira bill was introduced in 2001. Coins are issued in various denominations of 50 kobo and naira. The value of the naira has been reduced several times.

The Nigerian flag is divided into three equal vertical stripes. The central white stripe symbolizes peace and unity, while the two green bars stand for the country's agriculture. The flag was designed in 1958 by a Nigerian who was a student in London, England, at the time. It was flown for the first time when the country became independent in 1960.

The melody of Nigeria's national anthem was composed by Ben Odiase, director of music of the Nigerian Police Band. A national committee organized a competition to write the words to the anthem. The committee combined excerpts from the best five entries to create the anthem. It was adopted in 1978. Here are the words to the first verse:

Arise, O Compatriots
Arise, O compatriots,
Nigeria's call obey
To serve our fatherland
With love and strength and faith.
The labor of our heroes past
Shall never be in vain
To serve with heart and might
One nation bound in freedom, peace and unity.

 For a link to a site where you can listen to the Nigerian national anthem, "Arise, O Compatriots," go to vgsbooks.com.

Famous People

MOSHOOD ABIOLA (1937–1998) Born into poverty in Abeokuta, Abiola won a scholarship to the University of Glasgow in Scotland. After returning home, he worked his way up in business and became one of the country's wealthiest men. His public-speaking abilities made him a popular politician, and he was elected president in 1993. When the election was annulled, he fled the country. Returning in 1994, he declared himself president-elect but was imprisoned on charges of treason. Following President Abacha's death in 1998, people were anticipating Abiola's release, when he suddenly died. Although the official cause of death was a heart attack, many Nigerians regarded his death as suspicious.

CHINUA ACHEBE (b. 1930) One of Nigeria's most famous writers, Achebe was born in Ogidi and attended a university in Ibadan. He traveled widely as a young man and has taught English literature at several universities in the United States. He has written novels, short stories, and nonfiction books including *Things Fall Apart* and *The Trouble with Nigeria,* and he won the 1972 Commonwealth Poetry Prize.

NNAMDI AZIKIWE (1904–1996) This politician, journalist, and teacher, popularly known as Zik, was one of the chief architects of Nigerian independence. An Igbo born in Zungeru, he grew up in Nigeria and went to a university in the United States. When he returned to Nigeria in 1937 to fight colonialism, he set up a chain of newspapers and founded an important political party. He became the first Nigerian governor-general in 1960 and was president of the republic from 1963 to 1966.

PHILIP EMEAGWALI (b. 1954) Born in Akure, Emeagwali demonstrated brilliance in mathematics as a child. His opportunities to study, however, were limited. In 1967 his family joined thousands of refugees of the Biafran War, and his schooling was interrupted again when his family could not afford the tuition. But Emeagwali went on to earn degrees in science, engineering, and computer technology from U.S. universities. His pioneering ideas for a vast computer network that could make super-speedy calculations revolutionized the field and won him the computer world's most prestigious award. Emeagwali is often called a "father of the Internet," and his Nigerian heritage makes him a role model to many African children.

FELA KUTI (1938–1997) This Afro-beat musician was born in Abeokuta to an elite Yoruba family. He studied in England and went on to record more than fifty albums. His songs criticized the government, and he was imprisoned as a result. His death from AIDS made the disease real to many Nigerians for the first time.

FLORA NWAPA (1931–1993) Born in Oguta, Nwapa was a novelist who wrote about Igbo life from a woman's viewpoint. She began her career as a teacher, but following the Biafran civil war she worked as a government administrator in the field of health and social welfare. She wrote five novels, several volumes of short stories, and a book of poetry and formed a publishing company to publish African books.

OLUSEGUN OBASANJO (b. ca. 1937) The current president of Nigeria, Obasanjo was born in Abeokuta. He attended the Baptist Boys' High School and continued his education in the army, where he rose through the military ranks. After President Mohammed was killed, Obasanjo ruled Nigeria briefly, turning the government over to civilian rule in 1979. He then was a diplomat to the United Nations and a critic of the Abacha regime. With his election in 1999, he became the country's first civilian leader in fifteen years.

HAKEEM OLAJUWON (b. 1963) This towering athlete has been named one of the National Basketball Association's Fifty Greatest Players in NBA History. Born in Lagos, he played soccer as a youth and did not get interested in basketball until he was a teenager. He came to the United States to attend the University of Houston in Texas. Olajuwon was picked to play for the Houston Rockets in 1984, and in 2001 he moved to the Toronto Raptors. He plans to retire after the 2002–2003 season.

KEN SARO-WIWA (1941–1995) Born in Bori, a city in the Niger Delta region, this journalist, playwright, poet, and novelist became an outspoken critic of the Nigerian military government. He also protested against the environmental damage done to the Niger Delta by the Shell Nigeria oil company. In an unfair trial, a military court found him guilty of involvement in the murders of four Ogoni chiefs. Saro-Wiwa and several alleged conspirators were executed, despite an outcry by environmental and human rights organizations and governments around the world.

WOLE SOYINKA (b. 1934) This playwright, poet, novelist, and critic was the first African to receive the Nobel Prize for literature, awarded to him in 1986. Soyinka was born in Abeokuta and studied in Ibadan and in England. He founded an important Nigerian theater company and has taught literature, drama, and creative writing at universities in Nigeria and the United States. His play *King Baabu* is a satire that ridicules African dictators. Loosely based on Shakespeare's *Macbeth*, it premiered in Lagos in 2001.

ABEOKUTA This city, located north of Lagos, has a large granite rock formation with caves at its base. Called Olumo Rock, the site has great significance to several ethnic groups. Ceremonies marking the beginning of the yam harvest also take place at the rock every year.

ABUJA Built with oil revenues and grandiose plans, Abuja is the country's modern but half-empty capital city. Much of the city is laid out in a crescent form at the foot of Aso Rock, where the presidential complex, National Assembly, and Supreme Court are located. North of Abuja is Zuma Rock, a granite outcropping 980 feet (299 m) high and 0.6 miles long (1 km), one of Nigeria's best-known landmarks.

BAUCHI The tomb of Sir Alhaji Abubakar Tafawa Balewa, Nigeria's first prime minister, is located in the city of Bauchi. Balewa's personal belongings, on display at this national memorial, were chosen to portray his simplicity and humility. Visitors can also listen to a recording of Balewa's speech broadcast on Nigeria's first anniversary.

BRAZILIAN QUARTER The distinctive architecture seen in this Lagos neighborhood reflects a style that was common in Brazil. It was brought to Lagos by the descendants of Yoruba slaves who, after being freed, returned to their ancestral homeland from Brazil in the mid-1800s.

CALABAR This small, rainy city, set on a hillside overlooking the Calabar River, has a quiet charm. The former governor's residence has been turned into a museum that houses relics of the city's past, from prehistoric days to the slave trade, palm oil trade, and colonial period.

INTERNATIONAL INSTITUTE OF TROPICAL AGRICULTURE Founded in Ibadan in 1967, the institute hosts about eighty scientists from around the world. They study agricultural practices, plant health, and natural resource management. Research focuses on food crops such as yams, cassavas, plantains, soybeans, maize, and cowpeas.

KANO Kano is the oldest city in West Africa, located at the southern limit of the camel caravan trade route to North Africa. Local sights include the old city walls, the Emir's Palace, and the huge Central Mosque. Kano is still a busy commercial center, and its Kurmi Market is one of the busiest in Africa. Nearby are ancient dye pits where textile workers dip cloth into pots containing blue indigo dye.

OBA'S PALACE This mud-walled palace in Benin City, home to the traditional kings of Benin, houses bronze and ivory sculptures depicting the city's history and other examples of West African art. Some of the best pieces, however, are no longer in Nigeria. The Benin Bronzes—some two thousand statues and plaques—were taken to Britain after British troops captured Benin City in 1897. The bronzes are currently at the British Museum in London, England.

brackish: mixed saltwater and freshwater. Brackish water is often found in tidal rivers or coastal regions, such as the Niger Delta.

bride price: a sum paid to the family of the bride in a marriage arrangement. The payment of a bride price is a common practice in African societies. The bride price may range from bolts of cloth or livestock to thousands of naira. Some women refuse to take part in this practice because they do not want to be sold.

caliphate: the domain of a caliph, who is a secular and spiritual leader of Islam and considered a successor of Muhammad, the founder of Islam

cassava: also called manioc, a plant with a starchy and nutritious rootstock. Nigeria is one of the world's largest producers of cassava, which is ground into flour and used in baking.

coup d'état: the forceful overthrow or change in government by a small group. When a coup is carried out without injuries or death, it is called a bloodless coup.

cult: a system of religious beliefs and rituals

desertification: the destruction of the biological potential of land, leading to desertlike conditions

emir: a ruler or chief in an Islamic state. An emir's state or jurisdiction is called an **emirate.**

mangrove: a tropical tree or shrub that sends out many prop roots and forms dense masses of plants in saltwater

oracle: a shrine or person through whom a deity (a god or goddess) is believed to reveal knowledge. The followers of some traditional African religions in Nigeria consult oracles for advice.

pastoral: devoted to or based on livestock raising. The Fulani of Nigeria have traditionally followed a pastoral lifestyle.

polygyny: the practice of a man having more than one wife at a time. Related terms are monogamy, the practice of marrying only one person at a time, and polygamy, in which a spouse of either sex may have more than one mate at one time.

smelt: to melt or fuse ore, often involving a chemical change, in order to free the metal. Evidence of iron smelting in Nigeria goes back to the A.D. 400s.

subsistence agriculture: farming that provides all or almost all of the goods required by the farm family without any surplus for sale; farming that produces a minimum and often inadequate return to the farmer

Sunni: the mainstream branch of Islam that adheres to orthodox traditions and acknowledges the first four caliphs as rightful successors of Muhammad. Most Nigerian Muslims follow this branch of Islam.

Glossary

Selected Bibliography

Africana.com: Gateway to the Black World. 2000.
Website: <http://www.africana.com> **(April 1, 2002).**
This site offers articles from the *Encarta Africana* encyclopedia.

Barde, Barbara, and Susan Barkley. *African Cloth and Clothing.*
Toronto: The Canadian Museum of Carpets and Textiles, 1976.
This pamphlet provides information and history about African textiles.

"Country in Focus: Nigeria." *Africa Recovery Online.* **1999.**
Website: <http://www.un.org/ecosocdev/geninfo/afrec/vol13no1/jun99.htm>
(April 1, 2002).
This issue of the United Nations publication *Africa Recovery* features Nigeria.

Else, David, et al. *West Africa.* **Melbourne: Lonely Planet, 1999.**
This informative travel guide covers Nigeria and its neighbors.

Encyclopedia Britannica. 2002.
Website: <http://www.britannica.com> **(April 1, 2002).**
This site presents the full contents of Encyclopedia Britannica, including an entry on Nigeria.

Europa World Yearbook 2001. **Vol. II. London: Europa Publications, 2001.**
This source offers a comprehensive recent political history and useful statistics.

"Gateway to National Information on Land, Water, and Plant Nutrition." *Food and Agriculture Organization (FAO).* **2001.**
Website: <http://www.fao.org/ag/agl/swlwpnr/nigeria/home.htm> **(April 1, 2002).**
This page from the Food and Agriculture Organization of the United Nations provides information on Nigeria's land and water resources.

Maier, Karl. "Nigeria: Land of No Tomorrow." BBC News. 2000.
Website: <http://news.bbc.co.uk/hi/english/world/africa/newsid_879000/879903.stm>
(April 1, 2002).
This is one of several background articles on Nigeria from the BBC, including links to current news stories.

Maier, Karl. *This House Has Fallen: Midnight in Nigeria.* **New York: PublicAffairs, 2000.**
A journalist who has covered Africa for many years examines chaos and corruption in Nigeria.

Metz, Helen Chapin, ed. "Nigeria: A Country Study." *Library of Congress, Federal Research Division.* **1991.**
Website: <http://lcweb2.loc.gov/frd/cs/ngtoc.html> **(April 1, 2002).**
This Library of Congress report gives a good overview of the history, people, and economy of Nigeria.

Murray, Jocelyn. *Cultural Atlas of Africa.* **New York: Checkmark Books, 1998.**
This book presents an overview of current and historical arts in Nigeria and other African countries.

"Nigeria Environmental Profile." *UNEP.Net.* **2002.**
Website: <http://www.unep.net/profile/index.cfm?countrycode=NG&tab=200>
(April 1, 2002).
This site from the United Nations Environmental Programme (UNEP) presents an environmental profile of Nigeria with links to a list of species found in the country.

Okehie-Offoha, Marcellina Ulunma, and Matthew N. O. Sadiku, eds. *Ethnic and Cultural Diversity in Nigeria.* **Trenton: Africa World Press, 1996.**
This book offers detailed descriptions of seven major ethnic groups in Nigeria.

"PRB 2001 World Population Data Sheet." *Population Reference Bureau (PRB).* **2001.**
Website: <http://www.prb.org> **(April 1, 2002).**
This annual statistics sheet provides a wealth of data on Nigeria's population, birth and death rates, fertility rate, infant mortality rate, and other useful demographic information.

Reddy, Marlita A., ed. *Statistical Abstract of the World 1994.* **Detroit: Gale Research, 1994.**
This report provides useful facts and figures on Nigeria and other nations.

Turner, Barry, ed. *The Statesman's Yearbook 2002: The Politics, Cultures and Economies of the World.* **New York: Macmillan Press, 2001.**
This resource provides concise information on Nigerian history, climate, government, economy, and culture, including relevant statistics.

Willett, Frank. *African Art.* **New York: Thames and Hudson, 1993.**
This richly illustrated book describes West African masks, sculpture, and architecture.

World Book Encyclopedia 2000. **Chicago: World Book, 2000.**
This encyclopedia offers an article with an overview of Nigeria's history, geography, culture, and economy.

Achebe, Chinua. *Things Fall Apart.* **New York: Anchor Books, 1994.**
Achebe's story of an Igbo wrestler, his family, and his fellow villagers was originally published in 1958 but is still worth reading for insight into Igbo culture.

Adeeb, Hassan, and Bonnetta Adeeb. *Nigeria, One Nation, Many Cultures.* **Tarrytown, NY: Benchmark Books, 1996.**
This title offers a colorful description of life in Nigeria.

AIDS: A Threat to Rural Africa
Website: <http://www.fao.org/Focus/E/aids/aids1-e.htm>
This website describes the impact of AIDS on African women, children, and rural poverty.

Emecheta, Buchi. *The Bride Price.* **New York: George Braziller, 1976.**
A love story about an Igbo girl who falls in love with a man whose prosperous father was once a slave.

Finley, Carol. *The Art of African Masks.* **Minneapolis: Lerner Publications Company, 1998.**
This book explores the craft and meaning of masks from African nations, including Nigeria.

International Institute for Tropical Agriculture
Website: <http://www.iita.org>
This site includes articles about crops and farming systems in Africa.

Maier, Karl. *Into the House of the Ancestors: Inside the New Africa.* **New York: John Wiley and Sons, 1998.**
This overview of Africa at a crossroads between the traditional and the modern is very relevant to an understanding of Nigeria.

An Mbendi Profile: Nigeria, Oil and Gas Industry
Website: <http://mbendi.co.za/indy/oilg/af/ng/p0005.htm>
This site from Mbendi, an African business website, provides an outline of oil and gas industry in Nigeria.

Montgomery, Bertha Vining, and Constance Nabwire. *Cooking the West African Way.* **Minneapolis: Lerner Publications Company, 2002.**
This cultural cookbook presents recipes for a variety of authentic and traditional dishes from Nigeria and other West African nations, including special foods for holidays and festivals.

Motherland Nigeria
Website: <http://www.motherlandNigeria.com>
This fun and informative site, run by a Nigerian living in California, has lots of information on Nigerian food, fashions, ethnic groups, news, and the Nigerian diaspora.

NigeriaWEB
Website: <http://odili.net/nigeria.html>
NigeriaWEB's homepage has news headlines, sports, and links to various Nigerian websites.

Further Reading and Websites

Reader, John. *Africa: A Biography of the Continent.* New York: A. A. Knopf, 1998.
This beautifully written and informative book about the African continent puts Nigeria into historical context.

Rekela, George R. *Hakeem Olajuwon: Tower of Power.* Minneapolis: Lerner Publications Company, 1993.
This biography explores the life and career of Nigerian basketball player Hakeem Olajuwon.

Roll Back Malaria
Website: <http://mosquito.who.int/cgi-bin/rbm/countryprofile.jsp>
This website for the World Health Organization's Roll Back Malaria program allows visitors to search for information and updates on malaria in various countries.

Soyinka, Wole. *Aké: The Years of Childhood.* New York: Random House, 1981.
This title is an autobiography about the early childhood of the author Wole Soyinka.

The Story of Africa
Website: <http://www.bbc.co.uk/worldservice/africa/features/storyofafrica/index.shtml>
This site is a BBC feature on African history and culture.

United Nations Integrated Regional Information Network
Website: <http://www.reliefweb.int/IRIN/archive/nigeria.phtml>
News reports about Nigeria, especially regarding political and human rights issues, from IRIN, part of the United Nations Office for the Coordination of Humanitarian Affairs.

vgsbooks.com
Website: <http://www.vgsbooks.com>
Visit vgsbooks.com, the homepage of the Visual Geography Series®. You can get linked to all sorts of useful on-line information, including geographical, historical, demographic, cultural, and economic websites. The vgsbooks.com site is a great resource for late-breaking news and statistics.

The World Bank Group
Website: <www.worldbank.org>
Search the World Bank's website to find economic information and other data for countries and regions including Nigeria.

The World Book Encyclopedia of People and Places. Chicago: World Book, 2002.
This informative encyclopedia offers overviews of Nigeria and other countries.

Captions for photos appearing on cover and chapter openers:

Cover: Urban Fulani women stop on their way to market to pose for the camera. The women are using a traditional means of transporting goods, balancing the items on their heads. A ring placed on their heads helps stabilize the bowl-shaped containers.

pp. 4–5 These Nigerian schoolchildren rush excitedly out of school at the end of the day.

pp. 8–9 Mangrove trees rise up from a swamp in southwestern Nigeria near Lagos. The trees are slowly dying because of rising water levels in the swamp.

pp. 18–19 This ancient plaque is from the Oba's Palace. It shows an oba, or king, standing between two warriors.

pp. 34–35 Fulani hunters stalk game on the savanna. Members of Nigeria's Fulani ethnic group traditionally follow a nomadic lifestyle.

pp. 42–43 A masquerade dancer leads a group of revelers during an art festival in Enugu.

pp. 56–57 Workers inspect the piping of one of Nigeria's many oil rigs. This one is located near Port Harcourt. The flame that flickers in the background is produced by burning natural gas, a by-product of oil production.

Photo Acknowledgments

The images in this book are used with the permission of: © Giles Moberly/ Panos Pictures, pp. 4–5, 47; Ron Bell/PresentationMaps.com, pp. 6, 11; © Betty Press/Panos Pictures, pp. 7, 16–17, 36, 44, 59, 64–65; © Bruce Paton/Panos Pictures, pp. 8–9, 12, 37, 60, 61; © Victor Englebert, pp. 10, 13, 14, 51; The Art Archive/Antenna Gallery Dakar Senegal/Dagli Orti, pp. 18–19, 21; © Phil Porter, p. 20; © CORBIS, p. 22; © Hulton-Deutsch Collection/CORBIS, p. 26; © Hulton|Archive, pp. 27, 29; © GREEN-PEACE/CORBIS SYGMA, p. 30; © Marcus Rose/Panos Pictures, pp. 31, 46, 54, 58, 63; © Reuters NewMedia Inc./CORBIS, p. 32; © Frank L. Lambrecht, pp. 34–35, 39, 50 (bottom), 62; © TRIP/J. Okwesa, p. 38; © Giacomo Pirozzi/Panos Pictures, pp. 40–41, 52; © Dora Lambrecht, pp. 42–43, 49; © James Morris/Panos Pictures, p. 45 (right); © TRIP/J. Highet, pp. 45 (left), 53; The Art Archive/Rijksmuseum voor Volkenkunde Leiden (Leyden)/ Dagli Orti, p. 50 (top); © David Cannon/Getty Images, p. 55; © CAMPBELL WILLIAM/CORBIS SYGMA, pp. 56–57; Banknotes.com, pp. 68.

Cover photo: © Giles Moberly/ Panos Pictures

Back cover: NASA